GETTING TO CLOSING!

INSIDER INFORMATION TO HELP YOU GET A GOOD DEAL ON YOUR MORTGAGE

BY

CHERYL L. PECK

authorHOUSE®

AuthorHouse™
1663 Liberty Drive, Suite 200
Bloomington, IN 47403
www.authorhouse.com
Phone: 1-800-839-8640

First published by AuthorHouse 3/5/2009

ISBN: 978-1-4389-3683-3 (sc)
ISBN: 978-1-4389-3684-0 (hc)

Library of Congress Control Number: 2009901798

Printed in the United States of America
Bloomington, Indiana

This book is printed on acid-free paper.

Disclaimer

Every effort has been made to ensure the information presented in this book is accurate and complete as of the date published. Given the volatility of the mortgage industry, laws, regulations, and program requirements can and do change frequently. The recent crisis in the mortgage industry is causing many program changes. Always check with your lenders, attorneys, and other real estate professionals for current information and requirements.

Consult a tax professional for accurate information concerning the impact on your taxes of any action you are considering.

DEDICATION

This book is dedicated to my husband, Michael, who made my dream of owning my own business come true.

TABLE OF CONTENTS

INTRODUCTION

The application process for real estate mortgage financing can be mysterious and complex. Your documents are dropped into a black hole; your loan officer asks you for a lot of weird and seemingly, unreasonable stuff; your closing date is postponed; and when you finally get to closing, you must bring more money than you were originally told.

I became a mortgage broker because of the terrible experience I had purchasing my first home. The process was not explained to me; my phone calls were not returned; my interest rate was not locked as promised, causing me to have a higher rate; and my closing was delayed because my loan officer and processor forgot to send the appraisal to the underwriter. I learned that, unfortunately, this was not a unique experience.

I began my career after college as a collector for a financial institution, repossessing vehicles and foreclosing on houses. Next, I worked for the Department of Defense, first as a civil servant, later as a contractor. After my contract ended in 1997, I decided to start another career.

When I decided to become self-employed and was evaluating different options, I remembered my home loan experience. I figured that if I just paid attention to my clients, explained everything, and returned phone calls, I could give others a better experience than I had.

I started my mortgage broker business with no experience and little training, but I was committed to providing my clients the best customer service I could. I was the only employee and would close only one loan at a time, so I could make sure to do it right. At the height of the refinance boom, there were twelve other employees and we were closing more than seventy loans per month. We were the broker of choice for others in the industry, closing loans for attorneys and Realtors. We even closed loans for our competitors' relatives!

Although I made mistakes as I learned the business, I found that if you are giving your best effort, most people are forgiving and appreciate an honest effort on their behalf.

This book is a quick reference guide for those contemplating purchasing or refinancing residential real estate. It will help you understand and navigate through the application process, obtain the best deal possible, and get to closing with a minimum of stress. The information is presented based upon how an underwriter will view your file, and includes information I gave my clients throughout the process. I think it is important for you to understand what is involved in the mortgage loan process, which will help you to get a better deal with less stress.

The information in this book should help you be less dependent upon your loan officer to provide information you need to know and help you make good decisions on what, for most people, is one of the largest financial transactions you may ever make. God blessed me with a wonderful business and I am happy to have the opportunity to share what I learned during my ten years as a mortgage broker. I pray this book will be a blessing to you, giving you the knowledge you need to evaluate the programs and processes to obtain the best real estate financing possible.

CHAPTER 1

GENERAL INFORMATION

Whether you apply with a mortgage broker, mortgage lender, or a bank, the process is basically the same. You complete the application and sign disclosures with a loan officer (loan origination). Your loan officer is your point of contact with the lender. The file is given to the processor to collect and verify credit, income, and asset information needed for loan approval. The processor prepares the file for submission to the underwriter for approval. Preparing the file for underwriting includes ordering reports (credit, appraisal, title commitments, and insurance declarations) and obtaining verifications (employment, asset, and rent or mortgage payments). The processor will obtain initial loan approval using your initial application, income documents (usually latest W2 and pay stub). Most lenders have an automated Web site that allows electronic uploading and application approvals. This initial approval is sometimes known as a *pre-approval* because it is based on credit and income verification only, without other verifications and property information. Final approval is subject to employment verification; asset verification; no changes in income, debt, or credit; and the appraised value of the property. Most sellers and Realtors prefer that a potential buyer is pre-approved before they enter serious contract negotiations. No seller wants to take his or her property off the market for several weeks only to find the buyer cannot obtain financing. A prequalification is a less formal procedure, which does not necessarily require submission of supporting documentation.

Once the loan is submitted for approval, a credit report is usually ordered/obtained. Your credit report, including the credit scores, will affect the interest rate and loan terms for which you qualify.

The processor organizes the complete file, including income, asset, and liability documentation; employment and rent or mortgage verification(s); and other documents, including a credit report, sales contract (for purchases), appraisal, insurance declarations, title commitment, and disclosures.

After processing, the completed file is submitted to the lender's underwriter, who will issue final approval for the loan and authorize funding. Most lenders allow electronic submission of the file. The underwriter will issue a conditional approval: approved subject to the submission of additional requested documentation known as conditions. Conditions will be anything that was not submitted in the original file that the underwriter requires for final approval and funding. If you have ever obtained real estate financing before, you may remember being asked for additional documentation after you have been told your loan was approved.

Once the underwriter clears the conditions on the file, the processor can order the closing package and funds for the loan.

A mortgage broker works with several different wholesale lenders and has access to all the programs offered by them (like an independent insurance agent). Wholesale lenders do not work directly with the public, although many wholesale lenders have a retail side that does work directly with the public, such as Wells Fargo.

A mortgage banker works for a bank that funds mortgage loans and has access to the programs offered by his bank.

Lenders fund loans from "warehouse lines of credit," a lender's credit line from a warehouse lender. The funded loans are usually sold to one of two federally chartered shareholder-owned companies - Fannie Mae (Federal National Mortgage Association) and Freddie Mac (Federal Home Loan Mortgage Corporation) - to reduce the amount of the lender's outstanding credit, thereby allowing the lender to fund more mortgage loans.

Fannie Mae and Freddie Mac issue underwriting guidelines—criteria that real estate loan application packages must meet to be eligible for purchase by the respective organization. Guidelines govern credit criteria, allowable debt in relation to income, assets, and the property. All lenders who sell loans to these organizations must abide by the same underwriting guidelines. Any loans that do not meet the guidelines will not be eligible for purchase by Fannie Mae and/or Freddie Mac and will probably be declined by the lender unless they have other programs available and are willing to keep the loan "in-house."

Because of the well-publicized problems in the mortgage industry, the federal government took over the operation of both Fannie Mae and Freddie Mac in September 2008. Many loan programs have been discontinued, including sub-prime (for those with low credit scores), stated income programs (for those who cannot document income in the traditional ways), and 100 percent (no down payment) loans.

During the late nineties, Congress mandated that Fannie Mae and Freddie Mac lower criteria for the purchase of mortgages so that those with lower credit scores could be approved for mortgage loans. These individuals had a history of late payments or defaulting on loans, so it is not surprising that a large number defaulted on their mortgage loan payments. In addition, many lenders offered programs that allowed borrowers to take on more debt than they could afford. Some programs were misused, which is fraud, to approve people who could not afford the program. Stated income and pay option programs—discussed in Chapter 9, "Selecting the Loan Program"—are two examples of programs whose misuse added to the mortgage crisis.

Fannie Mae is a shareholder-owned company with a federal charter to buy real estate mortgage loans from banks and lenders to maximize the availability of mortgage funds to homeowners. The mortgages back securities that are sold to investors. This practice allows banks and lenders to clear out their warehouse lines of credit so that they have more money available to lend to other homeowners.

Freddie Mac is a similar program designed to help those with low and moderate incomes, including first-time home buyers, qualify for mortgage financing. Freddie Mac provides money for lenders to make mortgage loans readily available to the public.

Most of the lowest-rate loans are underwritten, approved, and funded under Fannie Mae or Freddie Mac guidelines. Guidelines for individual programs change. For current guidelines on specific programs, check with your lenders.

Programs designed to help specific groups qualify for mortgage loans include Federal Housing Administration (FHA)– and Veterans Administration (VA)–guaranteed loans.

The Federal Housing Administration (FHA) provides mortgage insurance on FHA loans made by approved lenders, which minimizes lender risk. This allows lenders to provide mortgage loans to people who may not otherwise qualify for a loan. The FHA programs require relatively low down payments and have flexible guidelines governing income requirements and debt ratios. The buyer pays private mortgage insurance, which allows the FHA to guarantee the loans made by the lenders.

The Veterans Administration (VA) guarantees mortgages requiring no down payment made by lenders to qualified veterans. The VA guarantees the loans made by approved lenders, allowing veterans access to favorable loan terms. The VA charges a funding fee, rather than private mortgage insurance, to the veteran homebuyer, which provides the funds for guaranteeing and buying back mortgage loans from the lenders in case of default by a veteran. The one-time funding fee may be (and usually is) rolled into the loan amount, even if the loan exceeds the sales price or appraised value of the house. The veteran obtains a Certificate of Eligibility from the Veterans Administration, which is required to obtain financing under the VA program.

A Veterans Administration loan is assumable with a qualified VA Certificate of Eligibility. Qualified veterans will have an eligibility certificate to qualify for the assumption of your loan. A nonveteran must use *your* Certificate of Eligibility in order to assume your loan. *Never allow someone to assume your loan using your Certificate of Eligibility. As long as your eligibility is on the loan, you are responsible. Any missed payments or defaults will show on your credit report.*

The FHA and VA lenders are approved by the respective organizations. The lender must approve individuals applying under FHA and VA programs. The FHA and VA do not approve or fund the loans; they guarantee the loans.

Sub-prime mortgage loans are loan programs for those with credit issues and lower credit scores, usually below 620 (see Chapter 12, "Your Credit"). Candidates for sub-prime mortgages cannot meet Fannie Mae or Freddie Mac guidelines and are ineligible for FHA and VA loans. Sub-prime mortgage rates are higher because the lender risk is higher. Sub-prime clients are those individuals who have had credit problems in the past, including late payments, collections, judgments from creditors, and bankruptcies.

Given the recent shake-up of the mortgage industry, sub-prime mortgage programs are not available. Many of the "A paper" (loan applications from those with good credit) programs have also been affected. Lower or zero down payment programs are hard to find and have stricter approval criteria.

Private Mortgage Insurance

Private Mortgage Insurance (PMI) is insurance that protects lenders from foreclosure losses on low down payment loans for purchases or low equity on refinances (less than 20 percent). The PMI helps minimize the risk a lender assumes in making a mortgage loan, allowing the lender to recover a portion of the investment should the borrower default on the loan and the property be foreclosed. The amount of the premium is determined by the risk involved (no down payment? purchase? refinance? payment history?). To calculate current PMI factors and premium amounts, check the Web site of PMI companies (www.mgic.com). The annual premium is divided by twelve and added to the monthly mortgage payment. Once you have acquired 20 percent equity in the property, through paying down the principal and property appreciation, you may request that the lender remove the PMI. The lender will probably require a new appraisal, which you must pay for. You must have a twenty-four-month payment history showing no late payments before you are eligible to have your PMI removed.

Beginning in 2007, PMI premiums may be tax deductible in some cases. Check the PMI (www.mgic.com) and Internal Revenue Service (IRS; www.irs.gov) Web sites for the latest details.

Using a second mortgage may avoid the requirement for PMI. Generally, PMI is not required if the first mortgage is 80 percent or less of the purchase price (purchase) or appraised value (refinance). The second mortgage will be the difference between the 80 percent first mortgage and the total loan amount required (second mortgage loan amount = sales price or appraised value minus 80 percent, minus down payment for purchases). Second mortgage interest rates are generally higher than first mortgage rates, so compare the costs of second mortgages and no PMI with a larger first mortgage and PMI, considering your tax situation.

The program changes made after the recent mortgage crisis have made second mortgages harder to obtain.

Real Estate Settlement Procedures Act (RESPA)

The Real Estate Settlement Procedures Act (RESPA) is a federal statute first passed in 1974 to protect consumers in the purchase of residential real estate. The statute requires specific disclosures be given to the buyer and restricts certain practices by real estate professionals. Required disclosures include: settlement (closing) costs, loan servicing practices (the percentage of loans the lender sells), and business relationships, if any, among service providers (does the lender or broker have a financial interest in the credit report company, appraisal company, title company, or other organization involved in the transaction?). The RESPA prohibits the payment of referral fees or kickbacks by real estate professionals (mortgage brokers, loan officers, processors, and Realtors, etc.) involved in the transaction.

The RESPA also says that the buyer chooses the closing attorney or title company used in the transaction as long as the lender approves the selection. Many Realtors and sellers think that if the seller pays closing costs, that the seller gets to choose. The logic behind the decision is that since the closing costs are coming out of the loan proceeds, the buyer is really paying and gets the choice of the closing attorney.

Note: The real estate closing attorney actually represents the lender, ensuring that all documents are correctly signed and funds are dispersed according to guidelines.

The RESPA is a complicated statute; this book only gives you a very brief overview. For more information, go to www.hud.gov.

CHAPTER 2

PURCHASES VERSUS REFINANCES

Although the process is similar for purchases and refinances, there are some fundamental differences. Purchases involve more people—buyers, sellers, and Realtors. More issues, schedules, and priorities must be considered, since more people are involved. Purchases are usually on tighter schedules, because, most of the time, both the buyers and sellers have moves, and maybe other closings, to coordinate.

Some closing costs (some lender fees and prepaid interest) are tax deductible. On purchases, the costs may be deducted in the year of the purchase. On refinances, they must be prorated over the life of the loan and deducted in increments. Check with a tax professional for current information.

Interest rates are the same for purchases and refinances.

Purchases

A purchase involves transferring the title from one party to another. The lowest-rate programs require a minimum of 5 percent of the sales price as a down payment for primary residences or second homes. These loan amounts can be as high as 95 percent loan-to-value (LTV), which is the

15

loan amount divided by the sales price. (The following is an example: sales price is $250,000; 5 percent down payment: $250,000 * 0.05 = $12,500; loan amount: $250,000 * 0.95 = $237,500; LTV = $237,500 / $250,000 = 0.95.) Purchases of investment properties require at least a 10 percent down payment. Purchases usually require the buyer to bring money to the closing. Funds for closing must come from an acceptable source (savings or tax refund, and *not* a cash advance on credit cards) as specified in the underwriting guidelines. Funds to close include the down payment; first year's homeowner's insurance premium; interest from the date of closing through the end of the month; and closing costs paid by the buyer, including lender and attorney fees, and at least half of the title insurance premium (some sales contracts state the seller pays half the title insurance premium). The amount of money you have available for closing will affect the program choice.

Closing costs paid by the buyer *cannot* be added into the loan on purchases. The seller can pay closing costs from the proceeds of the loan. If the seller pays closing costs, they have probably been built into the house's sales price. The appraised value of the house must support the sales price. (See Chapter 15, "The Appraisal, Title Work, and Homeowner's Insurance.")

Including the Spouse on the Loan and/or Deed

Many times, two-income families will need the income from both spouses to qualify for the loan. However, if the debt ratio is low and income from both spouses is not required for loan approval, both spouses are not required to be on the loan. The loan will be approved if the income submitted is sufficient to pay the mortgage loan payment, including taxes and insurance, as well as debt listed on the credit report within underwriting guidelines. Generally, the income aspect of the loan will be approved if the debt ratio is 40 percent or less. If one spouse has credit problems, leaving him/her off the loan can result in loan approval on a lower-rate and better-term loan program. Credit rating is an important consideration in the decision of whether or not to put a spouse on the loan. *The loan will be graded/approved based upon the lowest middle credit score.* If the spouse's income is not necessary for loan approval, the decision to place the spouse on the loan depends upon the credit rating as well as upon whether or not the spouse needs and/or wants the credit history of the mortgage on his/her credit report.

The spouse, or anyone else, can be on the deed without being on the loan. If the spouse, or anyone else, is on the loan, they *must* be on the deed.

If the spouse has court-ordered judgments on their credit report, which may result in liens being placed on the property after closing and recording the mortgage, it may be best to leave the spouse off the deed to avoid future issues. Those with legal issues should discuss their situation with a real estate attorney to determine the best way to proceed. *Note: On refinances, any judgments or liens on the property must be paid prior to funding the refinance transaction. If there is enough equity in the property, the judgments and liens may be paid through a cash-out transaction.*

Cosigners

Many clients asked me about having a family member cosign on the loan if they had credit or debt ratio problems. Since the loan is graded/approved based upon the lowest credit score, a cosigner will not improve the package's credit grade or interest rate. Also, the cosigner must qualify based on his/her debt ratio, including his/her current rent or mortgage payment, the new mortgage payment in this transaction, and any debt showing on his/her credit report. This can be difficult for some cosigners. I rarely closed loans with cosigners. Usually other programs will work for the buyer without using a cosigner. Most people prefer to obtain the mortgage loan themselves rather than asking a parent or other relative for help. If you are in this situation, I recommend you work to improve your financial and/or credit situation to be able to qualify on your own.

Lease Purchases

A lease purchase is a good way for buyers to live in the house until they are ready to close the purchase. In addition, many people like to lease the house for a period to make sure they want to buy the property. The lease purchase agreement specifies the sales price, the period of time the buyer/tenant has to exercise the option to purchase, the amount of rent paid prior to the purchase, and the terms of the rental agreement. The prospective buyer pays a deposit or earnest money, which is nonrefundable if the purchase option is not exercised. The amount of the deposit is negotiable between the buyer and seller. If any amount paid above the rent is to go toward the down payment, it must be specified in the agreement. The amount of rent must be reasonable for the market. An underwriter will disallow a low or zero rent payment with most or all of the money going toward the down payment. If the amount of rent looks reasonable given the purchase price of the house, the underwriter will not require additional documentation. The monthly rent/down payment contributions must be documented that they were paid, and paid on time, so do not pay by cash or money order. The lease purchase agreement will serve as the sales contract.

Dealing with Foreclosures

Purchasing foreclosures under market value can be a way to build equity quickly and is popular with investors. Financing foreclosures is more complicated than other purchases. Most foreclosures are sold "as is," which means the seller (usually the lender, who now possesses the property) will not make any necessary repairs. Unfortunately, some former owners leave the property damaged. Foreclosures usually need repairs to meet Fannie Mae and Freddie Mac guidelines. All repairs indicated in the appraisal must be completed before the property will be accepted as collateral on Fannie Mae or Freddie Mac loan programs. If the property needs work, you will have to use a rehabilitation (rehab) loan, or construction-type financing to purchase the property and get the deed in your name so work can begin. The rehab loan will lend an amount based upon the "subject to" value, or the value after repairs are made. Loan amounts and down payment requirements vary, so check with several lenders. Down payment requirements are usually higher on rehab loans. As a mortgage broker, I found that local banks are a good source for rehab money. Keep in mind that these programs will require you to have good credit. Rehab loan proceeds will be used to purchase the property (get the deed in your name) and finance the repairs. Once the repairs have been completed, the appraiser will reinspect the property and the loan will be converted to permanent financing by the rehab lender, or you can refinance with another lender. Many times, the rehab lender will have slightly higher interest rates but low or no closing costs. Review and compare the terms of available programs for permanent financing to determine the program and lender that are best for you. To compare program costs, determine the amount of closing costs for each program as well as the payment amount at the prevailing interest rate. Subtract the lower-interest-rate program payment from the higher-interest-rate program payment. Divide the answer by the amount of closing costs on the lower-rate program. The answer is the "break even point"—the number of months you must keep the mortgage to justify the expense of the closing costs to obtain a lower rate. If you do not plan to be in the house that long, a program offering a lower rate but higher closing costs might not be the best deal for you.

Example: $100,000 rehab loan must be refinanced.

Option 1: Convert loan to permanent financing by rehab lender at 7 percent, 30-year fixed, no closing costs. Principal and interest payment: $665.30

Option 2: Refinance with another lender at 6 percent, 30-year fixed, $3500 closing costs. Principal and interest payment: $599.55

Payment difference between Option 1 and Option 2: $65.75

Low-rate lender closing costs divided by payment difference: $3500/65.75 = 53.23 months. It will take almost four and a half years to recoup closing costs on the lower-rate program.

Note: Principal and interest payments can be determined by using a financial calculator. Also, many lender and Realtor Web sites have mortgage payment calculators. To determine a mortgage payment, you must have a loan amount, interest rate, and repayment period.

There are considerations other than interest versus closing costs, of course. Time in the property and tax impact should also be considered. Since you are allowed to roll closing costs into the loan when you refinance, you may not have out-of-pocket expenses other than the credit report and the appraisal.

This method can be used to compare other programs with varying interest rates and closing costs.

I had a client who found a great deal on a VA foreclosure that he intended to use as his primary residence. The property was to be sold "as is" and only needed about $500 of repairs to meet financing guidelines. The client was not able to get rehab financing due to his low credit scores. The client offered to pay for the repairs out of his pocket prior to closing, but the VA refused to give him access to the property because of liability considerations. The lender stood firm on completing the repairs prior to closing and would not let the $500 be escrowed for repairs post-closing. The client had to find another property and lost a good deal. *Those who deal in foreclosures need cash and good credit!*

Another consideration with foreclosures is the former owner's right of redemption. Some states allow the previous owner an amount of time (usually one year) to redeem his property, called the redemption period. This right is rarely exercised, because the previous owner must buy back the property and usually is not in a position to do so. Some lenders will fund purchases of foreclosures still in the redemption period if the title company will issue a redemption bond (the premium is included in the closing costs). Some lenders will not fund a foreclosure purchase at all until the property is out of the redemption period. If you are dealing with a foreclosure, check with your state to determine if there is a redemption period and with your lender for how they handle redemption periods.

Refinances
Rate/Term versus Cash Out

A transaction is considered a refinance if at least one original titleholder (owner of the property) remains on the deed. A rate/term refinance will pay off the existing loan and allow you to roll in closing costs. A cash-out refinance will pay off the existing mortgage plus closing costs and take equity out as cash or to pay off consumer debt. A transaction to pay a former spouse their share of equity in the subject property and remove them from the deed would be considered a cash-out refinance.

Many times, clients who were shopping for rates told me that my competitors quoted them a higher rate for a refinance than for a purchase. Although there are conditions that affect rates (see Chapter 11, "Locking an Interest Rate"), most lenders do not charge higher rates for a refinance than for a purchase.

There are some differences in the loan terms and underwriting requirements in rate/term and cash-out refinances, including loan-to-value limits, interest rates, and maximum dollar amount of cash out. *For refinances, loan-to-value equals loan amount divided by appraised value rather than the sales price for purchases. If you have an estimate of your property value, multiply it by the LTV percentage to determine the amount you can borrow. Rate/term refinance transactions allow a 95 percent LTV; cash-out transactions allow a 90 percent LTV. If your home appraises for $350,000, you could have a loan amount of $332,500 on a rate/term transaction ($350,000 * 0.95) and $315,000 on a cash-out transaction ($350,000 * 0.90).* Using the appraised value of the property allows you to take advantage of the equity in the property.

By federal law, refinances of primary residences (does not apply to investment property) have a three-day right of rescission, which is the ability to cancel the transaction. Funds will not be released until after midnight of the third day. You can cancel the transaction during this three-day period, by signing and submitting a cancellation form to the closing attorney. You should be given a copy of this form at closing. Weekdays and Saturdays are counted as rescission days. Funding days are business days only—no Saturdays. Sundays and holidays are never counted for either a rescission or a funding day. If you sign the closing package on Thursday, your rescission period is Friday, Saturday, and Monday. Your loan will fund on Tuesday.

A *rate/term* refinance occurs when you are paying off a first mortgage and rolling in the closing costs. Paying off a second mortgage can be considered rate/term *if* it is a fixed-rate second or a home equity line of credit (HELOC) that was used to purchase the home and *no additional draws have been made after closing*. If a HELOC is being paid through a rate/term refinance, an underwriter will usually require a copy of the settlement statement (the closing document detailing closing costs and who pays them) from the purchase to document that it originated during the original purchase transaction. On a rate/term refinance, you can receive the lesser of $2,000 or 2 percent of the loan amount in cash at closing. If you receive more cash than the lesser of $2,000 or 2 percent of the loan amount, the loan will be reclassified as a *cash out* and must be resubmitted to underwriting; possibly delaying the closing.

A *cash-out refinance* allows you to "cash out" equity in the property to pay off consumer debt or receive cash.

When you're paying off consumer debt, the payoffs may be made by the attorney or title company at funding and shown on the settlement statement, or the cash may be given directly you. If the debts are paid at closing, they are marked on the application as being paid at closing and not counted in the debt ratio. These debts must be paid by the attorney at closing to keep the debt ratio the same as for the loan approval. Give your loan officer copies of the latest statements on accounts to be paid off so they can be submitted to the attorney. If you will receive more than $20,000 cash out, the underwriter will require a letter of explanation

(LOE) from you stating what you intend to do with the cash. Some underwriters/programs require the LOE for lesser amounts. *The LOE should be general—pay off debt, home improvement, pay for college, etc., without going into a lot of detail, which may raise additional underwriting questions.*

Closing costs may be rolled into a refinance loan only. On a purchase, the sales price may be increased and the contract state that the seller is paying all or a portion of the closing costs. Even though that sounds like rolling in closing costs, on a purchase, the seller is allowed to pay closing costs, but the buyer is not allowed to roll them into the loan.

If a property has been listed for sale within the last twelve months, Fannie Mae and Freddie Mac guidelines prohibit the refinancing.

I never got a good answer for why you cannot refinance a property that has been listed for sale in the past year. I was told by an underwriter that the owner would be more likely to walk away from the property, although that would seem to be more a function of the owner's credit rather than whether or not they had previously tried to sell the property.

When Should You Refinance?

The decision to refinance depends upon a number of factors: interest rates, number of years you intend to own the property, closing costs versus decrease in payment amount, the need to take equity out of the property in cash. Compare the difference in payments between the two interest rates. Be sure to consider principal and interest only—do not include taxes and insurance, which will stay the same. If you have had your original loan for a considerable period, the principal amount may be significantly lower, which will lower the payment amount. Taking cash out will increase the principal amount, which will raise your payment.

Request a Good Faith Estimate (GFE) to review the estimate of closing costs. Divide the closing costs by the payment difference in your current and prospective loans, if your payment will go down. The resulting number is the number of months you must have the loan before you "break even" or recoup your closing costs by lower payments. You should always consider closing costs along with interest rates when you make your decision on whether or not to refinance.

If you have had your loan a long time and interest rates have dropped significantly, refinancing may be a good strategy. However, chasing the lowest rate is not a good idea. Closing costs can negate the savings realized from a lower interest rate, and you may be adding years to your loan. When rates were dropping rapidly, I had a few clients who insisted on refinancing a couple of times a year. Sometimes, I could talk them out of it by showing them how closing costs negated their savings at a lower interest rate. Sometimes, the client was so determined to have a rate lower than his friends and colleagues that he did not care about closing costs, especially since they were rolled into the loan and not an out-of-pocket expense. This is not a smart way to manage your finances!

Taking Equity Out of Your Property in Cash

The decision to take cash out of your property should be made only after serious consideration. Your home is probably your largest asset and should be protected. Taking the equity out of your home to remodel and increase the value is one valid reason for a cash-out refinance. I do not believe that cashing in your equity to pay off other debt is a good idea, even though mortgage interest rates are lower than those for consumer loans. Cash-out refinances to pay off other consumer debt without changing spending habits will put you even further in the hole financially, because you will eventually acquire more consumer debt. I believe a more effective way to eliminate debt is the old-fashioned way—exercise self-discipline to stop spending, live on a budget, and develop a good financial management plan. There are good books and DVDs on financial management and debt reduction designed to help get you started.

Other reasons people cash in equity are for investment opportunities (bad idea), to pay for college (you should save and pay as you go), or to take a vacation (absolutely worst idea).

Taking the maximum amount of cash out of your property may put you in a bad position if the real estate market in your area drops. You may find you owe more on your house than the amount for which it will appraise. Your home is not the place for risky financial transactions!

CHAPTER 3

POSITION YOURSELF
FOR A GOOD DEAL

How the Underwriter Will View Your Application

The underwriter will review your application package and make the final approval decision. The underwriter ensures the application package meets the lender's guidelines.

The lowest rate and best terms for mortgage financing require good credit (high credit scores of at least 720), low debt in relation to income (debt ratio), and assets (money in the bank). Your loan officer or processor will request documents to verify your employment, income, and assets. Employment and income will be verified for the past two years. Assets will be verified for the past sixty days.

Employment

An underwriter looks for a stable employment history. Frequent job changes over the past two years may adversely affect your approval decision. Current jobs with temporary employment agencies will usually not be allowed; *the loan will not be approved until you have permanent employment.* Once you have permanent employment, you can count the temporary job in your two-year employment history. The underwriter does not like to see gaps in employment. You must explain any gaps in employment over thirty days. If you have less than two years' employment history but you are a recent graduate of a university or trade school and are working in your field of study, an underwriter will generally accept your employment if you provide a copy of your diploma and school transcripts for review. Remember to include any part-time jobs you had while you were in school.

Income

For approval purposes, gross income (before taxes) is used. An explanation of how to calculate income is presented in Chapter 7, "Completing the Application," in the income section. You can count income you are actually receiving, not future income. If you are expecting a raise in three months or are starting a new job with a higher salary, you cannot count that income until you actually receive the first paycheck with the new income.

Rent

If you are currently renting where you live, some programs require you to document that rent payments were made *on time* (rent was never more than thirty days late) for the past twelve months. If you rent from a property management company, a written verification of rent from the company is usually accepted. Many people rent from an individual who prefers cash. *Cash rent payments cannot be documented and will not be accepted by the underwriter. Written receipts for cash or money orders will not be accepted.* If you rent from an individual, you should **always** *pay by check* so each payment can be documented.

This also applies if you have a seller-financed mortgage that is not reported on your credit report. You cannot document cash or money order payments to an individual.

The application requires you to list your address for the past two years, but rent or mortgage verification will be required for only one year.

Assets

Two months' statements on all accounts (bank accounts, stocks, bonds, mutual funds, and retirement accounts) will document your assets. Asset documentation is required when you are bringing money to closing, usually on purchases. You must document that you have the money to close. In addition, some programs require that you have reserves (assets), usually an amount equaling two months' mortgage payments (principal, interest, taxes, and insurance) in a liquid account. Assets include savings and checking accounts; stocks, money market, or mutual funds; and retirement accounts. The more assets you have, the stronger your application. High asset values will also help you get loan approval if you have a high debt ratio, minimizing risk to the lender. If you have large deposits within the last sixty days, the underwriter will ask for documentation to verify the source of the funds to ensure it meets guidelines. Examples of valid sources of funds include savings in other accounts in your name, tax refunds, gifts from a relative, and loans from your retirement account.

Credit

Your credit is crucial to your approval decision as well as to the rate and terms for which you will qualify. Your loan will be approved based on your credit scores and debt ratio (minimum monthly payments divided by gross monthly income). With the tighter criteria for real estate loan approval that have been recently put in place, credit scores and debt ratios are more important than ever.

Many people have a problem with too much debt in relation to their income. *Credit should be used as a convenience, not to finance a lifestyle you cannot otherwise afford.* I believe credit card balances should be paid off monthly. Do not charge more than you can afford to pay. For expensive items, save the money to pay for them, then purchase paying cash. Paying off debt takes discipline and responsibility. Having little or no debt eliminates one of life's biggest stresses! There are many good books, CDs, and DVDs on the market on how to develop the discipline required to pay off debt and that offer debt-reducing strategies and methods.

For a more detailed discussion on credit and debt, see Chapter 12, "Your Credit."

CHAPTER 4

CHOOSING A LENDER

Most residential real estate loans are sold to either Fannie Mae or Freddie Mac (see Chapter 1, "General Information"), so the loan program guidelines should be the same regardless of the lender. If you have good credit, you will be able to qualify for the lowest rates. In addition to rates, your main priorities in choosing a lender should be the character, integrity, and customer service of the loan officer and processor. Another consideration is lender fees, which will vary.

Call several lenders to ask for rates and a Good Faith Estimate, which will disclose lender fees and other closing costs. Be prepared to explain your situation: purchase or refinance, down payment amount if a purchase, either cash out or rate/term if a refinance, loan size, and general credit information (excellent, some minor issues, etc.). Most rates are quoted as a base rate. There are add-ons for different loan types, amounts, and situations. (See Chapter 11, "Locking an Interest Rate.") When you are calling lenders, *do not give any of them your social security number or allow them to run a credit report.* You should allow only the lender you have selected to handle your loan to run your credit report. Loan officers may tell you they must know your credit before they can quote you a rate, but at this stage you are just checking for the rates they offer—you are not asking them to guarantee *your* rate or approval. Running multiple credit reports that will not be used can lower your credit score. You run an increased risk of identity theft if you have multiple credit reports with your social security number floating around.

Your ideal loan officer should be knowledgeable and helpful without pressuring you. He or she should return phone calls and e-mails promptly. I was amazed at the number of loans I closed simply because I was the only one who returned the potential clients' calls! If a loan officer does not return your call when you are shopping around, you can be sure you will not hear from them once they have your business! So mark them off your list!

During your conversations with prospective loan officers, ask them to e-mail you a Good Faith Estimate, with the interest rate included. The GFE will show you the closing costs for each lender. If you encounter any hesitation from a loan officer about sending you their GFE, move on! You do not want to deal with a loan officer who is unwilling to provide you an itemization of costs you will incur at closing! Compare the GFEs of several lenders to get an idea of closing costs that seem reasonable and those that seem high.

Remember to compare interest rates along with closing costs. If rates and closing costs vary significantly among lenders, you can use the method described in the section on purchasing foreclosures in Chapter 2, "Purchases versus Refinances," to help you make a decision on which lender and program to use.

As you can see, the interest rate is only one consideration. Most rates do not vary a great deal from lender to lender. It may be worth an eighth, or even a quarter, of a point to have a loan officer who provides great service, honest information, and low closing costs!

CHAPTER 5

GETTING STARTED WITH THE PROCESS

Understanding the requirements for the property and what documents you will need to provide will speed up the entire process, from application submission through closing.

Property Use and Type

The property use and type will influence the selection of the mortgage loan program. The property use will affect the down payment requirements and interest rates. Property use may also trigger some underwriting requirements. (For example, owning multiple investment properties requires you to demonstrate two years' property management experience if you manage the properties yourself.) Most programs have property-type restrictions, so always make sure that the subject property will fit within the selected program guidelines.

Property Use

- Primary residence—you reside there at least 51 percent of the time

- Second home—vacation or otherwise occupied less than 50

percent; is not rented to others

- Investment—produces (or you intend to produce) rental income

Property Type

- Single-family residence
- Condominium
  - ○ Low-rise (equal to or less than four stories high)
  - ○ High-rise (more than four stories high)
  - ○ Warrantable? (considers such information as percent of complex complete versus still under construction; percent of investors versus primary residences in the complex)
- Town house
- Duplex
- Fourplex (a fourplex is the largest number of units allowed on residential loan programs)
- Apartment (requires a commercial loan)
- Manufactured or modular home
- Log home
- Is the property a foreclosure?

Note: Many loan programs do not allow manufactured or log homes. The programs/lenders that do allow these unique properties require the appraiser to provide comparable sales of similar properties (log home or manufactured home sales) within a specified distance. This can be difficult or impossible, which will cause the loan to be declined. *Be sure to tell your loan officer about your property type as soon as you know. If the loan officer discovers an unusual property type after the appraiser has begun the appraisal, you may owe the fee just to find out your loan has been declined due to the property type.*

Documents You Should Bring to the Application Interview

Having your documentation with you at the initial interview will speed up your approval process. You should bring these documents with you when you meet with your loan officer. Your loan officer will copy them and give the copies to the processor to begin your file.

Purchases

- Copy of the sales contract (if available) (see Chapter 14, "The Real Estate Sales Contract")

- Full income documentation
  - Previous two years' W2s and latest pay stub
  - Award letters and bank statements showing deposits for social security and retirement income
  - For the self-employed, or those relying on investment income to qualify, provide two year's federal tax returns with all schedules—everything you submitted to the Internal Revenue Service

- Asset documentation—statements covering sixty days on all accounts

- Copy of your driver's license or other government-issued picture ID

- Names and contact numbers for the verbal verification of employment prior to closing

- Be prepared to pay the fees for the credit report and

appraisal—ask your loan officer the amount of the fees and when they should be paid

Refinances

- Full income documentation
  - o Previous two years' W2s and latest pay stub
  - o Award letters and bank statements showing deposits for social security and retirement income
  - o For the self-employed, or those relying on investment income to qualify, provide two years' federal tax returns with all schedules—everything you submitted to the Internal Revenue Service
- Asset documentation, if you are bringing in funds to closing
- Copy of your driver's license or other government-issued picture ID
- Names and contact numbers for the verbal verification of employment (VOE) prior to closing
- Be prepared to pay the fees for the credit report and the appraisal—ask your loan officer the amount of the fees and when they should be paid
- Copy of deed of the property to be refinanced
- Copy of monthly mortgage statement or payment coupon (to request loan payoff)
- Copy of insurance declarations page (summary page issued each year)
- Copy of title insurance policy, if available (from purchase closing)

- Copy of any current credit card or loan statements to be paid by the refinance

Other Documentation, If Applicable, for Both Purchases and Refinances

- Investment property leases for all property you own

- Divorce decree (all pages) (only if it affects your finances—you pay or receive alimony or child support)

- Bankruptcy papers (all pages)

- Gift letter (if your down payment is a gift from a relative) which states the relative's name, relationship to you, *amount of gift that does not have to be repaid)*

On refinances, submitting the deed, mortgage statement, and insurance declarations page will speed the processing time. Providing these documents to the attorney, title company, appraiser, and your insurance agent allows them to provide the processor with the required documentation faster. The mortgage statement or payment coupon gives the attorney/title company the information required to order the payoff on the existing mortgage(s).

If you purchased owner's title insurance when you bought your home, the attorney/title company may be able to reissue the existing policy rather than writing a new policy. Reissuing the existing policy could save you as much as 40 percent of the title insurance premium. If you are not sure if you have a title insurance policy, check the settlement statement from the original purchase. Under the section for attorney fees, there will be a line for title insurance. If there is an amount by owner's premium, you have the insurance and should look in your files for the policy.

If your loan officer does not mention your option to reissue the title policy, be sure to ask them to check with the closing attorney!

CHAPTER 6

THE APPLICATION INTERVIEW

The initial interview is much more than taking the application. It is an opportunity to get to know your loan officer, let him/her know what your priorities are (lowest rate, minimum out-of-pocket costs), and identify any issues that could affect the program selection and loan approval. Your loan officer should explain the process, costs, and responsibilities to you. Most people are not very familiar with the real estate loan process. Even those who are not first-time homebuyers do not buy and sell real estate often enough to remember everything that goes on. Purchasing real estate involves a lot of money and legal procedures which can be very intimidating. Remember, you are the client and you deserve respect and honest treatment. Do not hesitate to ask questions or request additional information. If you are not comfortable with the information provided or the people you are working with, go somewhere else!

Most lenders have secure Web sites that allow you to complete your application online. Doing this will save you time in the lender's office and give the loan officer time to generate a more accurate Good Faith Estimate and Truth-in-Lending disclosures based upon your situation. Your loan officer will make sure you have completed the application and will present/explain the required disclosures.

If you do not already know the loan program you want—30-year fixed-rate, 15-year fixed-rate, adjustable-rate, etc.—your loan officer can give you information to help you decide the program that is best for you.

Most loan officers will collect the credit report fee during the initial interview. When you make the appointment, ask what fees and amounts must be paid up front.

The appraisal also has a fee that usually is collected before the report is ordered. The loan officer is responsible for paying the credit report and appraisal fees regardless of whether or not the loan closes, so most of them will collect the fees from you early. On purchases where the seller is paying closing, you will be reimbursed for the fees at closing.

Remember to tell your loan officer if you prefer to use a particular appraiser and closing attorney. You, as the client, have the right to choose your appraiser and attorney as long as the lender will approve them. Most lenders will approve anyone who does not have a history of problems and complaints.

Information to Give to Your Lender Refinancing FHA Loans

On refinances, if you are paying off an FHA loan, be sure to tell your loan officer. The FHA lender must receive the payoff funds by the first day of the month at 1:00 PM lender's time. Closing should be planned accordingly, and your loan officer should notify all parties involved.

Refinancing with Second Mortgages

If you are refinancing and have a second mortgage, let your loan officer know if you want to pay it off in this transaction. *Remember,* if the second is a home equity line of credit, the transaction *may* be treated as a cash-out refinance (see the section on refinances in Chapter 2). The amount of the existing second will affect the total loan-to-value and may affect the program. Loan programs have limits on how high the loan-to-value can be. If the second mortgage is a HELOC and is to be left open, *the amount considered in the LTV is the HELOC ceiling, not the current principal balance.* If a second is to be left open rather than paid off, the lender will require a subordination agreement to allow the current second to remain in second place after the refinance. *Most second mortgage lenders charge a fee to generate the subordination agreement. If so, be prepared to pay it up front or order the subordination agreement directly from the second mortgage lender yourself.*

Unusual Property Types

Manufactured homes, log cabins, and condominiums, as well as all unusual properties, have specific underwriting requirements that may be difficult to meet. Be sure your loan officer is aware of any unusual property types involved in the transaction.

Escrow Accounts

Let your loan officer know whether you want an escrow account for your property taxes and homeowner's insurance premium. Most lenders will set up an account at no charge to you to collect monthly property tax and homeowner's insurance premium payments. The property tax bill and annual homeowner's insurance premium are divided by twelve and added to the loan's principal and interest payment. Each year when the property taxes and homeowner's insurance premium are due, the mortgage company pays them from the money in the escrow account. Establishing an escrow account for the collection of money for taxes and insurance is usually optional. Determine if you want the taxes and insurance collected as part of the payment each month and paid by the lender when due. *You may have to pay a slightly higher interest rate if you do not escrow, so be sure to ask your loan officer the effect on your interest rate if you decide not to escrow.* The amount of money collected at closing to start the escrow account, along with interest collected from the date of funding through the end of the month, are called prepaids because you are paying them in advance. Prepaids may be rolled into the loan on a refinance but not a purchase. See section e, "Estimate Prepaid Items under Details of Transaction," page 4 of the application.

First-time homebuyers or those without many assets should strongly consider taking advantage of the escrow accounts. There are many examples where new homeowners lose or almost lose their home to foreclosure because they did not have escrows collected by the lender and did not have the money to pay the taxes and insurance when due.

Chapter 7

Completing the Application

Most lenders' Web sites allow you to complete an online application. You will save time in the lender's office and will expedite the approval process if you do. Real estate mortgage forms are standard in the United States. The application, disclosures, and closing documents will provide the same information regardless of which lender you use or in which state you close. Complete the application as thoroughly as possible. Some information is required for an initial approval. Additional information provided will help the processor expedite your application process.

For initial loan approval, you may estimate income, assets, and liabilities. Be prepared to document income and assets. For initial approval, your loan officer will probably request at least your latest pay stub. The liability section of the application will be changed to reflect the credit report. The initial approval basically looks at your credit score and debt ratio. The only documentation that is required is a pay stub. This will be enough to generate an initial approval letter for your Realtor or seller.

For final loan approval, asset and other verifications are required.

The following loan application is a standard form required for all real estate loan application packages. You can print blank forms from several sites on the Internet.

Uniform Residential Loan Application

This application is designed to be completed by the applicant(s) with the Lender's assistance. Applicants should complete this form as "Borrower" or "Co-Borrower," as applicable. Co-Borrower information must also be provided (and the appropriate box checked) when ☐ the income or assets of a person other than the Borrower (including the Borrower's spouse) will be used as a basis for loan qualification or ☐ the income or assets of the Borrower's spouse or other person who has community property rights pursuant to state law will not be used as a basis for loan qualification, but his or her liabilities must be considered because the spouse or other person has community property rights pursuant to applicable law and Borrower resides in a community property state, the security property is located in a community property state, or the Borrower is relying on other property located in a community property state as a basis for repayment of the loan.

If this is an application for joint credit, Borrower and Co-Borrower each agree that we intend to apply for joint credit (sign below):

Borrower _____ Co-Borrower _____

I. TYPE OF MORTGAGE AND TERMS OF LOAN

Mortgage Applied for:	☐ VA ☐ FHA	☐ Conventional ☐ USDA/Rural Housing Service	☐ Other (explain):	Agency Case Number	Lender Case Number
Amount $	Interest Rate %	No. of Months	Amortization Type:	☐ Fixed Rate ☐ GPM	☐ Other (explain): ☐ ARM (type):

II. PROPERTY INFORMATION AND PURPOSE OF LOAN

Subject Property Address (street, city, state & ZIP)		No. of Units
Legal Description of Subject Property (attach description if necessary)		Year Built

Purpose of Loan	☐ Purchase ☐ Construction ☐ Refinance ☐ Construction-Permanent	☐ Other (explain):	Property will be: ☐ Primary Residence ☐ Secondary Residence ☐ Investment

Complete this line if construction or construction-permanent loan.

Year Lot Acquired	Original Cost $	Amount Existing Liens $	(a) Present Value of Lot $	(b) Cost of Improvements $	Total (a + b) $ 0.00

Complete this line if this is a refinance loan.

Year Acquired	Original Cost $	Amount Existing Liens $	Purpose of Refinance	Describe Improvements ☐ made ☐ to be made Cost: $

Title will be held in what Name(s)	Manner in which Title will be held	Estate will be held in: ☐ Fee Simple ☐ Leasehold (show expiration date)
Source of Down Payment, Settlement Charges, and/or Subordinate Financing (explain)		

III. BORROWER INFORMATION

Borrower	Co-Borrower
Borrower's Name (include Jr. or Sr. if applicable)	Co-Borrower's Name (include Jr. or Sr. if applicable)

Social Security Number	Home Phone (incl. area code)	DOB (mm/dd/yyyy)	Yrs. School	Social Security Number	Home Phone (incl. area code)	DOB (mm/dd/yyyy)	Yrs. School

☐ Married ☐ Unmarried (include ☐ Separated single, divorced, widowed)	Dependents (not listed by Co-Borrower) no. ages	☐ Married ☐ Unmarried (include ☐ Separated single, divorced, widowed)	Dependents (not listed by Borrower) no. ages
Present Address (street, city, state, ZIP) ☐ Own ☐ Rent ____ No. Yrs.		Present Address (street, city, state, ZIP) ☐ Own ☐ Rent ____ No. Yrs.	
Mailing Address, if different from Present Address		Mailing Address, if different from Present Address	

If residing at present address for less than two years, complete the following:

Former Address (street, city, state, ZIP) ☐ Own ☐ Rent ____ No. Yrs.	Former Address (street, city, state, ZIP) ☐ Own ☐ Rent ____ No. Yrs.

IV. EMPLOYMENT INFORMATION

Borrower	Co-Borrower

Name & Address of Employer	☐ Self Employed	Yrs. on this job	Name & Address of Employer	☐ Self Employed	Yrs. on this job
		Yrs. employed in this line of work/profession			Yrs. employed in this line of work/profession
Position/Title/Type of Business	Business Phone (incl. area code)		Position/Title/Type of Business	Business Phone (incl. area code)	

If employed in current position for less than two years or if currently employed in more than one position, complete the following:

	Borrower		IV. EMPLOYMENT INFORMATION (cont'd)		Co-Borrower	
Name & Address of Employer	☐ Self Employed	Dates (from – to)	Name & Address of Employer	☐ Self Employed	Dates (from – to)	
		Monthly Income $			Monthly Income $	
Position/Title/Type of Business	Business Phone (incl. area code)		Position/Title/Type of Business	Business Phone (incl. area code)		
Name & Address of Employer	☐ Self Employed	Dates (from – to)	Name & Address of Employer	☐ Self Employed	Dates (from – to)	
		Monthly Income $			Monthly Income $	
Position/Title/Type of Business	Business Phone (incl. area code)		Position/Title/Type of Business	Business Phone (incl. area code)		

V. MONTHLY INCOME AND COMBINED HOUSING EXPENSE INFORMATION

Gross Monthly Income	Borrower	Co-Borrower	Total	Combined Monthly Housing Expense	Present	Proposed
Base Empl. Income*	$	$	$ 0.00	Rent	$	
Overtime			0.00	First Mortgage (P&I)		$
Bonuses			0.00	Other Financing (P&I)		
Commissions			0.00	Hazard Insurance		
Dividends/Interest			0.00	Real Estate Taxes		
Net Rental Income			0.00	Mortgage Insurance		
Other (before completing, see the notice in "describe other income," below)			0.00	Homeowner Assn. Dues		
				Other:		
Total	$ 0.00	$ 0.00	$ 0.00	Total	$ 0.00	$ 0.00

* Self Employed Borrower(s) may be required to provide additional documentation such as tax returns and financial statements.

Describe Other Income

Notice: Alimony, child support, or separate maintenance income need not be revealed if the Borrower (B) or Co-Borrower (C) does not choose to have it considered for repaying this loan.

B/C		Monthly Amount
		$

VI. ASSETS AND LIABILITIES

This Statement and any applicable supporting schedules may be completed jointly by both married and unmarried Co-Borrowers if their assets and liabilities are sufficiently joined so that the Statement can be meaningfully and fairly presented on a combined basis; otherwise, separate Statements and Schedules are required. If the Co-Borrower section was completed about a non-applicant spouse or other person, this Statement and supporting schedules must be completed about that spouse or other person also.

Completed ☐ Jointly ☐ Not Jointly

ASSETS Description	Cash or Market Value	Liabilities and Pledged Assets. List the creditor's name, address, and account number for all outstanding debts, including automobile loans, revolving charge accounts, real estate loans, alimony, child support, stock pledges, etc. Use continuation sheet, if necessary. Indicate by (*) those liabilities, which will be satisfied upon sale of real estate owned or upon refinancing of the subject property.		
Cash deposit toward purchase held by:	$			
List checking and savings accounts below		**LIABILITIES**	Monthly Payment & Months Left to Pay	Unpaid Balance
Name and address of Bank, S&L, or Credit Union		Name and address of Company	$ Payment/Months	$
Acct. no.	$	Acct. no.		
Name and address of Bank, S&L, or Credit Union		Name and address of Company	$ Payment/Months	$
Acct. no.	$	Acct. no.		
Name and address of Bank, S&L, or Credit Union		Name and address of Company	$ Payment/Months	$
Acct. no.	$	Acct. no.		

Name and address of Bank, S&L, or Credit Union		Name and address of Company	$ Payment/Months	$
Acct. no.	$	Acct. no.		
Stocks & Bonds (Company name/ number & description)	$	Name and address of Company	$ Payment/Months	$
		Acct. no.		
Life insurance net cash value	$	Name and address of Company	$ Payment/Months	$
Face amount: $				
Subtotal Liquid Assets	$ 0.00			
Real estate owned (enter market value from schedule of real estate owned)	$			
Vested interest in retirement fund	$			
Net worth of business(es) owned (attach financial statement)	$	Acct. no.		
Automobiles owned (make and year)	$	Alimony/Child Support/Separate Maintenance Payments Owed to	$	
Other Assets (itemize)	$	Job-Related Expense (child care, union dues, etc.)	$	
		Total Monthly Payments	$	
Total Assets a.	$ 0.00	Net Worth (a minus b) ▶ $ 0.00	Total Liabilities b.	$ 0.00

Schedule of Real Estate Owned (If additional properties are owned, use continuation sheet.)

Property Address (enter S if sold, PS if pending sale or R if rental being held for income) ▼	Type of Property	Present Market Value	Amount of Mortgages & Liens	Gross Rental Income	Mortgage Payments	Insurance, Maintenance, Taxes & Misc.	Net Rental Income
		$	$	$	$	$	$
Totals		$ 0.00	$ 0.00	$ 0.00	$ 0.00	$ 0.00	$

List any additional names under which credit has previously been received and indicate appropriate creditor name(s) and account number(s):

Alternate Name	Creditor Name	Account Number

VII. DETAILS OF TRANSACTION		VIII. DECLARATIONS				

	VII. DETAILS OF TRANSACTION		VIII. DECLARATIONS	Borrower		Co-Borrower	
			If you answer "Yes" to any questions a through i, please use continuation sheet for explanation.	Yes	No	Yes	No
a.	Purchase price	$					
b.	Alterations, improvements, repairs		a. Are there any outstanding judgments against you?	☐	☐	☐	☐
c.	Land (if acquired separately)		b. Have you been declared bankrupt within the past 7 years?	☐	☐	☐	☐
d.	Refinance (incl. debts to be paid off)		c. Have you had property foreclosed upon or given title or deed in lieu thereof in the last 7 years?	☐	☐	☐	☐
e.	Estimated prepaid items		d. Are you a party to a lawsuit?	☐	☐	☐	☐
f.	Estimated closing costs		e. Have you directly or indirectly been obligated on any loan which resulted in foreclosure, transfer of title in lieu of foreclosure, or judgment?	☐	☐	☐	☐
g.	PMI, MIP, Funding Fee		(This would include such loans as home mortgage loans, SBA loans, home improvement loans, educational loans, manufactured (mobile) home loans, any mortgage, financial obligation, bond, or loan guarantee. If "Yes," provide details, including date, name, and address of Lender, FHA or VA case number, if any, and reasons for the action.)				
h.	Discount (if Borrower will pay)						
i.	Total costs (add items a through h)	0.00					

VII. DETAILS OF TRANSACTION		VIII. DECLARATIONS					
j.	Subordinate financing		If you answer "Yes" to any questions a through i, please use continuation sheet for explanation.	**Borrower**		**Co-Borrower**	
				Yes No		Yes No	
k.	Borrower's closing costs paid by Seller		f. Are you presently delinquent or in default on any Federal debt or any other loan, mortgage, financial obligation, bond, or loan guarantee? If "Yes," give details as described in the preceding question.	☐ ☐		☐ ☐	
l.	Other Credits (explain)		g. Are you obligated to pay alimony, child support, or separate maintenance?	☐ ☐		☐ ☐	
			h. Is any part of the down payment borrowed?	☐ ☐		☐ ☐	
m.	Loan amount (exclude PMI, MIP, Funding Fee financed)		i. Are you a co-maker or endorser on a note?	☐ ☐		☐ ☐	
			j. Are you a U.S. citizen?	☐ ☐		☐ ☐	
n.	PMI, MIP, Funding Fee financed		k. Are you a permanent resident alien?	☐ ☐		☐ ☐	
			l. Do you intend to occupy the property as your primary residence? If "Yes," complete question m below.	☐ ☐		☐ ☐	
o.	Loan amount (add m & n)	0.00	m. Have you had an ownership interest in a property in the last three years?	☐ ☐		☐ ☐	
p.	Cash from/to Borrower (subtract j, k, l & o from i)		(1) What type of property did you own—principal residence (PR), second home (SH), or investment property (IP)? (2) How did you hold title to the home—solely by yourself (S), jointly with your spouse (SP), or jointly with another person (O)?	——— ———		——— ———	

IX. ACKNOWLEDGEMENT AND AGREEMENT

Each of the undersigned specifically represents to Lender and to Lender's actual or potential agents, brokers, processors, attorneys, insurers, servicers, successors and assigns and agrees and acknowledges that: (1) the information provided in this application is true and correct as of the date set forth opposite my signature and that any intentional or negligent misrepresentation of this information contained in this application may result in civil liability, including monetary damages, to any person who may suffer any loss due to reliance upon any misrepresentation that I have made on this application, and/or in criminal penalties including, but not limited to, fine or imprisonment or both under the provisions of Title 18, United States Code, Sec. 1001, et seq.; (2) the loan requested pursuant to this application (the "Loan") will be secured by a mortgage or deed of trust on the property described in this application; (3) the property will not be used for any illegal or prohibited purpose or use; (4) all statements made in this application are made for the purpose of obtaining a residential mortgage loan; (5) the property will be occupied as indicated in this application; (6) the Lender, its servicers, successors or assigns may retain the original and/or an electronic record of this application, whether or not the Loan is approved; (7) the Lender and its agents, brokers, insurers, servicers, successors, and assigns may continuously rely on the information contained in the application, and I am obligated to amend and/or supplement the information provided in this application if any of the material facts that I have represented herein should change prior to closing of the Loan; (8) in the event that my payments on the Loan become delinquent, the Lender, its servicers, successors or assigns may, in addition to any other rights and remedies that it may have relating to such delinquency, report my name and account information to one or more consumer reporting agencies; (9) ownership of the Loan and/or administration of the Loan account may be transferred with such notice as may be required by law; (10) neither Lender nor its agents, brokers, insurers, servicers, successors or assigns has made any representation or warranty, express or implied, to me regarding the property or the condition or value of the property; and (11) my transmission of this application as an "electronic record" containing my "electronic signature," as those terms are defined in applicable federal and/or state laws (excluding audio and video recordings), or my facsimile transmission of this application containing a facsimile of my signature, shall be as effective, enforceable and valid as if a paper version of this application were delivered containing my original written signature.

Acknowledgement. Each of the undersigned hereby acknowledges that any owner of the Loan, its servicers, successors and assigns, may verify or reverify any information contained in this application or obtain any information or data relating to the Loan, for any legitimate business purpose through any source, including a source named in this application or a consumer reporting agency.

Borrower's Signature	Date	Co-Borrower's Signature	Date
X		X	

X. INFORMATION FOR GOVERNMENT MONITORING PURPOSES

The following information is requested by the Federal Government for certain types of loans related to a dwelling in order to monitor the lender's compliance with equal credit opportunity, fair housing and home mortgage disclosure laws. You are not required to furnish this information, but are encouraged to do so. The law provides that a lender may not discriminate either on the basis of this information, or on whether you choose to furnish it. If you furnish the information, please provide both ethnicity and race. For race, you may check more than one designation. If you do not furnish ethnicity, race, or sex, under Federal regulations, this lender is required to note the information on the basis of visual observation and surname if you have made this application in person. If you do not wish to furnish the information, please check the box below. (Lender must review the above material to assure that the disclosures satisfy all requirements to which the lender is subject under applicable state law for the particular type of loan applied for.)

BORROWER ☐ I do not wish to furnish this information		CO-BORROWER ☐ I do not wish to furnish this information	
Ethnicity: ☐ Hispanic or Latino ☐ Not Hispanic or Latino		Ethnicity: ☐ Hispanic or Latino ☐ Not Hispanic or Latino	
Race: ☐ American Indian or Alaska Native ☐ Asian ☐ Black or African American ☐ Native Hawaiian or Other Pacific Islander ☐ White		Race: ☐ American Indian or Alaska Native ☐ Asian ☐ Black or African American ☐ Native Hawaiian or Other Pacific Islander ☐ White	
Sex: ☐ Female ☐ Male		Sex: ☐ Female ☐ Male	
To be Completed by Interviewer This application was taken by: ☐ Face-to-face interview ☐ Mail ☐ Telephone ☐ Internet	Interviewer's Name (print or type) Interviewer's Signature Date Interviewer's Phone Number (incl. area code)	Name and Address of Interviewer's Employer	

CONTINUATION SHEET/RESIDENTIAL LOAN APPLICATION

Use this continuation sheet if you need more space to complete the Residential Loan Application. Mark B f or Borrower or C for Co-Borrower.	Borrower:	Agency Case Number:
	Co-Borrower:	Lender Case Number:

I/We fully understand that it is a Federal crime punishable by fine or imprisonment, or both, to knowingly make any false statements concerning any of the above facts as applicable under the provisions of Title 18, United States Code, Section 1001, et seq.

Borrower's Signature	Date	Co-Borrower's Signature	Date
X		X	

The Application

Page 1

Complete each section as completely as possible. The final application, which you will sign at closing, will have information based upon the final numbers: loan amount, interest rate, closing costs, liabilities, assets, etc.

I. Type of Mortgage and Terms of Loan. Complete these sections as thoroughly as possible: type: (conventional, VA, FHA, USDA/Rural Housing), loan amount, interest rate, number of months, fixed or adjustable rate. If you are not sure about the loan types, you can leave this blank and discuss the available programs with your loan officer. The lender if necessary will provide the agency case number and lender case number. The loan amount can be an estimate at this point. You should have an idea of the price range for a purchase and a loan amount for a refinance. The important point here is to list an appropriate initial amount for the initial loan approval. You can leave the interest rate blank. The processor will use a market rate for the initial approval. List the number of months you are considering for your repayment period (360 for a thirty-year loan; 180 for a fifteen-year loan). On the initial application, mark "fixed rate" for amortization type. On the initial application, you just need to give the loan officer and processor enough general information to get an idea of what you want to do so they can get an initial approval. The details will be added later.

II. Property Information and Purpose of Loan. List the subject property address, number of units, year built, legal description (if unknown put "see title"), purpose, and property use. If you are being pre-approved for a purchase and do not yet know the property address, put "TBD" (to be determined). For refinances, if you have the year built and legal description, add it, but if you do not have it readily available, the processor can add the information on the final application.

If you are applying for a construction/permanent loan, list year lot acquired, original cost, amount of existing liens, present value of lot, and cost of improvements. If you are applying for a loan that will purchase the lot, leave these sections blank but include the lot price in the loan amount in section I.

If the transaction is a refinance, enter the appropriate information. You can estimate the amount of the existing loan(s). The processor will enter the actual loan amount once the credit report is obtained.

<u>Title</u>: List the names to be on the deed/title and manner in which title will be held or vesting (unmarried man, husband and wife, etc.). On a refinance, the names on the title generally do not change (unless a divorce is involved). You should complete the application using the names that appear on the deed—initials for middle name, complete middle name, maiden name, etc. On purchases, be sure to tell your loan officer how the name(s) should be listed on the title. Be aware that if a married person is listed alone on the title for the primary residence, the spouse may be required to sign some of the closing documents (mortgage, truth-in-lending, etc.). A person can be on the deed without being on the loan/note. The reverse is not true. If a person is on the loan/note, they must be on the deed.

In the section "estate will be held in:" either check "fee simple" or leave blank. How you hold title to the property is a legal issue. If you have special circumstances, you should discuss your situation with a real estate attorney. Most people will hold title as "fee simple". Fee simple is the highest form of real estate ownership recognized by law. The owner has full rights to the property, limited only by zoning laws, deed restrictions, or restrictions from subdivisions or covenants.

III. Borrower Information. Complete this section as thoroughly as possible. Some information, such as name, social security number, and birth date, is required. Provide two years' address of primary residence information. *The address must be a street address and not a post office box. The post office box can be listed as a mailing address. If you rent,* *do you rent from a property management company or pay an individual by check?* Some programs require twelve months' cancelled rent checks if the landlord is an individual. *Rent payments in cash or money order to an individual landlord cannot be documented.* An underwriter will not accept receipts from an individual landlord to document cash rent payments. If a property management company collects the rent, cash payments are acceptable. The property management company will complete a verification of rent. The ability to document rent payments may affect the choice of loan program.

IV. Employment Information. List your current employer's address and phone number.

Page 2

IV. Employment Information cont. List the name and address of previous employers, if necessary to cover a two-year period. Frequent job changes over a two-year period indicate job instability and raise a red flag to an underwriter, who may look closer at the file before issuing an approval. Remember, most loan programs will not allow you to close if you are employed through a temporary agency. Once you obtain permanent employment, you may use the temporary employment as part of your two-year job history. For current employment, be prepared to give your loan officer the name and phone number of several coworkers who can verify employment. Most lenders require their closing department employees to call for a verbal verification of employment before the closing package is released. If the closer cannot contact anyone, the closing may be delayed. Usually, the closer will only ask if you are still employed, so the contact does not have to know hire dates, salary, etc. I provided the underwriter with two or three contacts for the verbal VOE so that the release of the closing package would not be delayed if a contact could not be reached. The closers must ensure the borrower still has income prior to funding the loan. I had several clients through the years who quit their job or were laid off between application and closing. You cannot close if the closer cannot verify your employment prior to the release of the closing package.

Changing employers during this process could delay closing. Most lenders require that you have received one paycheck before closing. If you must change jobs before you close, tell your loan officer as soon as possible.

V. Monthly Income and Combined Housing Expense Information.

Gross Monthly Income. Input the base income based on the W2s and pay stub showing year-to-date income provided. The income amount used is gross (before taxes). To calculate base income:

1. Hourly rate * number of hours per pay period * number of pay periods per year / 12 = gross monthly income

    (Example: $24 per hour, paid biweekly: 24 * 80 = $1,920 * 26 = $49,920 annual / 12 = $4,160 per month.) Note: *Do not* use four weeks per month, since you will understate income.

2. Annual, according to your W2, divided by 12 = gross monthly income

Overtime, bonuses, commission, rental income, dividend/interest income may be used only if you have been receiving it for two years (documented by federal tax returns) or verification of employment and the extra income is likely to continue. If the overtime or commission income is not the same each month, average the last twenty-four months to use for approval.

Retirement/social security income is listed under "other" income. Documentation must show you are: (1) entitled to receive the income (award letter), and (2) actually receive the income (most have the money direct-deposited into their bank accounts, so two months' statements showing the deposits are usually enough documentation to count the income).

Alimony or child support income is documented by providing the complete divorce decree. For child support, the age or birth dates of the children should be listed; otherwise, you will have to provide birth certificates or other documentation of the children's ages. To use alimony or child support income, the income must continue for three years from the loan closing date. Some loan programs, especially sub-prime programs, require documentation that the borrower is actually receiving the alimony or child support payments. Sometimes this is difficult or impossible to provide if the transaction does not involve an outside agency (court-administered or payroll-deducted by employer). If the exact amount is not deposited each time in the bank account, bank statements cannot document payments. Providing canceled checks (front and back) will document the payments, if the former spouse is willing to provide them.

Self-employment income is documented with two years' federal tax returns, including all schedules. Guidelines require that you be self-employed at least two years before the loan can be approved. Many self-employed people cannot document adequate income from tax returns. Previously, this would require a stated income program, which did not document income, but these have been discontinued.

Note: Stated income programs are no longer allowed under Fannie Mae and Freddie Mac guidelines.

A person operating a *sole proprietorship* will show business income and deductions with a 1040 Schedule C Profit or Loss from Business. Net profit (or loss) (line 31) for the last two years divided by twenty-four is used for monthly income for loan approval. Financial statements from a certified public accountant (CPA) will document year-to-date income for the current year. If you do not use a CPA or use a bookkeeper who is not a CPA, you will have a problem documenting year-to-date income, because underwriters will not accept financial statements from anyone other than a CPA.

If you have depreciation listed on the Schedule C, the amount of the depreciation should be added to the net income, since depreciation is not a cash expense.

Real estate investment income is shown on 1040 Schedule E, Supplemental Income and Loss. Income, or loss, is shown on line 26, Total rental real estate or royalty income (or loss). Divide by twelve for monthly income/loss.

If you are self-employed and have ownership interest in a corporation or partnership, you should provide your loan officer or processor your Schedule K-1, along with your federal tax returns.

If you have an ownership interest in a corporation or limited liability company (LLC) (also reports individual shares of company profits on a Schedule K Form 1065) and have W2 income from the company, you can count the W2 income if you have been receiving it for at least two years. You will need the standard income documentation of W2s and latest pay stub. You will also need the tax returns with the Schedule Ks included, because you are still considered self-employed if you have at least a 25 percent ownership interest in the company.

When tax returns are provided to document income, you must sign both the copy of the 1040 form and a 4506-T, which allows the lender to order your tax returns from the Internal Revenue Service. *Be aware that many lenders require the underwriter to automatically order the return from the IRS and compare it to the forms you submitted in the loan application package.* A discrepancy in the two forms is considered client fraud.

In the past, most self-employed people used stated income programs because they could not document sufficient income for loan approval. Stated income programs have been discontinued given the current situation in the mortgage industry. (Note: Stated income programs were designed for those who could not document income in the traditional ways. *They were not* designed as an opportunity to make up income that did not exist!) It is unethical, irresponsible, and illegal to overstate income just to get the loan approved. Some sub-prime programs used twelve to twenty-four months of bank statements and averaged the deposits to determine self-employment income, but rates were usually significantly higher.

Dividends/interest. Unless this is a significant part of your income, leave blank.

Net rental income. Net rental income (you can only count 75 percent of monthly rent; 25 percent is considered set aside for repairs and maintenance) will be calculated from information added under "Schedule of Real Estate Owned" on page 3 of the application. If 75 percent of the rent is more than the mortgage payment—including taxes, insurance, and any association dues—of the rental property, net rent will be positive and counted as income. If the mortgage payment,(including taxes, insurance, and association dues) is more than 75 percent of the rent, net rent will be negative. The negative amount will be counted in the debt ratio. *You will probably be asked to provide mortgage statements or payment coupons for each investment property to document that property taxes and insurance are included in the payment. Otherwise, you must document the amount of taxes and insurance, which will be added to your debt ratio.*

If you have multiple investment properties, you will usually have to document rental income to qualify for your transaction approval. Rental income documentation includes a lease and the latest two years of IRS Schedule E. You can also include two years' IRS Schedule E forms to document two years of property management experience.

Note: If you have multiple rental properties and you are using rental income for loan approval, a minimum of two years' property management experience is required. (Submitting two years of Schedule E from the tax returns will qualify.) If you use a professional property management company (not your own), the two years' experience requirement is waived.

Monthly housing expenses. List existing rent or mortgage payments on your primary residence, including second mortgage, if any. List "included" on the lines for taxes and insurance if your mortgage payment includes taxes and insurance. You do not have to complete the proposed housing expenses section; the processor's application software should calculate principal and interest payments based upon the loan information provided. The processor will add the amount of taxes and insurance. If there are monthly homeowner's association dues, those will also be added because they affect the debt ratio. If the new mortgage payment is significantly higher than the current mortgage or rent payment, the difference is considered to be "payment shock." The underwriter will look closely at your credit, income, and debt to be sure you will be able to handle an increased amount of debt. If the loan amount is more than 80 percent of the appraised value (refinances) or sales price (purchases), private mortgage insurance will apply. Private mortgage insurance rates may be calculated from www.mgic.com. *Some debt ratios are so close to approval ceilings, that taxes and/or insurance may affect the approval.*

V1. Assets and Liabilities.

Assets. On purchases, assets must be documented showing funds to close. Documentation should cover sixty days. Any large deposits must be documented and explained. I always advised clients with few assets to start building savings as soon as possible once they decided to buy a house to make sure they had the required funds and to make sure they were "seasoned" (at least sixty days old). For refinances, if you are financing the total outstanding mortgage balance and rolling closing costs into the loan, no asset documentation is required. If you are paying down the mortgage balance or bringing in closing costs, documentation of funds to close is required.

Fannie Mae and Freddie Mac underwriting guidelines also have requirements/restrictions on the source of funds to close. If the money has been in your account for sixty days, it is automatically sourced and seasoned. (Sourced: where the money came from; seasoned: how long the money has been in your bank account.) If not, you must document where/how you obtained the funds to close. Some programs allow a gift from a relative (immediate family). Other acceptable sources include selling an asset, advances on salary and/or commission, tax refunds, borrowing from your retirement account, or equity in existing property. Be sure to tell your loan officer if you are having trouble documenting your assets. I had a client who sold a motorcycle for the down payment on his house. The underwriter required not only the bill of sale (which could be easily produced) but also the registration of the bike in the new owner's name. Fortunately, the buyer was a friend of the client, so it was easy to get. If the source of funds is other than savings or a gift, be sure to check with your loan officer to determine what documentation is required.

The amount of money you have available for down payment and closing costs will affect the program options available to you. The lowest-rate programs require a minimum of 5 percent down payment. It is extremely important to discuss funds required for closing during the initial interview to determine how much is available and *where it is coming from.* If you are just beginning the search for a home, you should have time to build some assets for closing. I would tell clients to start putting as much money as possible into one account as soon as possible and to avoid any unnecessary expenses. If a major expense comes up unexpectedly after your loan has been approved, you should call your loan officer to discuss the impact on the loan application.

Most programs limit the amount of funds a seller can contribute to closing. Called seller concessions, closing costs are usually described as a percentage of the sales price. The lowest-rate, 95 percent programs *allow seller concessions up to 3 percent of the sales price for primary residences and 2 percent for investment property. Many times, buyers, sellers, and Realtors are not aware of the lower amount sellers are allowed to contribute to closing costs on the purchase of investment property.* You may want to revise the terms of your contract given the program restrictions on seller concessions.

Liabilities. You should list all debt on the initial application. For loan approval, the liability section must match the credit report, so your processor will revise your final application to reflect the credit report. Any liability that appears on the credit report but not on the initial application should be discussed with you. If the debt has been paid, you should be able to provide documentation. Debt that will be paid within ten months, according to the credit report (ten payments are greater than or equal to the balance), do not have to be counted. Any debt that will be paid off with this transaction (cash-out refinance) should be noted by checking the "will be paid" box. Any new debt incurred before the closing/funding of this loan may result in your loan being declined. You should avoid any new debt. If circumstances require new debt (you need a new car to get to work), you should call your loan officer first to determine the impact on their loan approval. Ideally, you should wait until after closing to incur new debt. If the debt is unavoidable, the loan must be reassessed given the additional debt.

Verifying rent or mortgage payments not shown on the credit report. If you rent from a property management company, a completed verification of rent form is usually enough to document on-time rent payments. If you are renting from an individual, twelve months' cancelled checks may required. Most landlords prefer cash, so it may not be possible to document rent. This is important to discuss with your loan officer during the initial interview, because it can affect the choice of loan program. Some programs do not require rent to be verified, especially if your credit score is high (720 or above).

Page 3

V1. Assets and Liabilities cont.

Other liabilities. Alimony and child support paid are liabilities documented by the *entire* divorce decree.

Schedule of real estate owned. Enter the subject property information first if the transaction is a refinance. List the primary residence ahead of investment property. On purchase transactions of primary residences, if you have a current primary residence to sell, *do not* put PS (pending sale) in the disposition box unless the house will be sold prior to closing on this transaction. A "PS" will require a settlement statement showing the property was sold and the mortgage was paid off prior to closing on this transaction. Just because the house is on the market does not make it a pending sale! Note: if the current primary residence will not be sold before closing on this transaction, the mortgage payment must be considered in the debt ratio. If the current residence will be sold prior to closing on this transaction, mark PS, which means the current mortgage payments will not be counted in the debt ratio. The underwriter will require a copy of the settlement statement prior to clearing of the file for closing to document the sale and the availability of funds for down payment and closing costs in this transaction. The settlement statement on the sale of the previous residence is considered valid documentation of sourced and seasoned funds.

Multiple mortgaged properties. List all properties on the schedule of real estate owned section. *To make it easier for the underwriter and the processors, cross-reference the properties and mortgages by putting the address of the property under the creditor's name in the liability section. Also, list the creditor's name by the property in the remarks section of real estate owned. Your processor may ask you for copies of mortgage statements on any mortgaged property that is not being paid by this transaction. The underwriter will want to see that the total payment includes taxes and insurance. Otherwise, you will have to document and count the taxes and insurance as additional debt.*

Non-mortgaged properties. For real estate that has no liens (mortgages), an underwriter will require documentation that property owned with no creditor on the credit report is not privately financed. If the property has a structure on it, an insurance declarations page showing no mortgagee clause will usually suffice. A vacant lot requiring no insurance is harder to document. An underwriter may take property tax documentation (unimproved property taxes are obviously lower than those for improved property). If proper documentation is not provided, an underwriter may require a title search from your attorney or title company on the property, which is costly and time consuming.

V11 Details of Transaction.

You do not have to complete the details of transaction section on your initial application. The processor's application system will generate data for the final application.

a. Purchase Price. Total sales price taken from the sales contract. If you are getting pre-approved prior to making an offer on a house, tell your loan officer the high end of the price range you are considering.

b. Alterations. Estimated cost of improvements (for new

59

construction or home improvement loans). This box will not be used for most purchases.

c. Land. Cost of the lot (construction or lot loans).

d. Refinance. The total amount of debt to be refinanced, including first and second mortgages and other consumer debt. If you have checked the "will be paid off" box in the liability section, the total is automatically calculated for you.

e. Estimated prepaid items. If these amounts are correct on the GFE, most processing software systems will automatically include the amount here. Prepaid items consist of interest from date of funding through the end of the month and homeowner's insurance premiums. On purchases, the first year's homeowner's insurance premium is collected at closing. I also added three months' insurance premiums and three months' property taxes to the escrow account for the cushion. On refinances, check the current insurance declarations page to determine the policy premium due date. Count the number of mortgage payments collected between the funding date and the premium due date. The difference of the premium amount less the amount collected in payments prior to the due date, plus the three months' cushion, will be collected at closing. This amount will usually be a high enough estimate to ensure you do not have to bring money to closing.

f. Estimated closing costs. This will be calculated automatically on your final application.

g. PMI, MIP, funding fee. Private mortgage insurance (PMI) and Monthly Insurance Premium (MIP) rates may be estimated by using the Web site www.mgic.com. PMI and MIP are the same fee with different names. Funding fees, which eliminate PMI requirements, are required on VA loans. Check with your loan officer for current factors for the funding fees.

h. <u>Discount (if borrower will pay)</u>. The amount of any points (a point is 1 percent of the loan amount) charged to buy the rate down.

i. <u>Total costs</u>. This field is automatically calculated.

j. <u>Subordinate financing</u>. The amount of an existing or new second mortgage is listed here.

VIII. Declarations. Answer questions *a* through *m* as thoroughly as possible. A "yes" answer for questions *a* through *g* requires an explanation on page 5. Review your answers to make sure they are correct. For some reason, a frequent mistake is marking "yes" to both "Are you a permanent resident alien?" and "Are you a U.S. citizen?" Once, a young first-time homebuyer marked "yes" to the question, "Have you had an ownership interest in a property in the last three years?" I reminded him he had never owned a home before. He said no, but he had an interest in owning a home!

If you are not a U.S. citizen, provide a copy (front and back) of your "green card" or visa. There are many different types of visas. Each loan program will specify which visas are required for a noncitizen to purchase property in the United States, so ask your loan officer.

Page 4

V11 Details of transaction cont.

k. <u>Closing costs paid by seller</u>. For purchases. (Obviously!) The amount of closing costs the seller will pay according to the contract goes here. Remember the amount of seller-paid closing costs is restricted depending upon the specific mortgage program you are using.

l. <u>Other credits</u>. Any money paid by you outside of closing will be listed here. This can include earnest money and appraisal and credit report fees.

m. Loan amount. The amount of the loan in this transaction.

n. PMI, MIP financed. The amount, if any, that is included in the loan.

o. Loan Amount—(m + n)

p. Cash from/to borrower. Most loan programs will not allow a buyer to receive cash at closing from the seller on a purchase. If the program was a no-down-payment program, you paid earnest money, and the seller paid all the closing costs, it is possible for you to receive money back that you paid outside of closing. An accurate estimate of all fees will give you an idea if you should expect to receive any money back. On a rate/term refinance, you can receive up to 2 percent of the loan amount or $2,000, whichever is less at funding. On a cash-out refinance, the amount of cash you can receive will be stated in the program requirements. An accurate GFE, including taxes and insurance information, will ensure an accurate amount you should expect to bring to closing, so be sure to check with your loan officer or processor prior to closing for a final estimate of closing costs. You can request a final settlement statement twenty-four hours prior to closing. I strongly recommend you do this. You will be able to review the closing costs to make sure they are close to what you were told, and you will know the exact amount, if any, you must bring to closing.

IX. Information for Government Monitoring Purposes.

If you check the box next to, "I do not wish to furnish this information," be aware that by federal law, the loan officer who takes the application must complete Section IX to the best of their ability. The answer is used to compile statistics on who applies for loans along with approvals and declines. This information is not used in the approval process. Those involved in closing your transaction—including mortgage lenders, Realtors, and attorneys—are not paid until your loan closes. It is not in anyone's best interest to discriminate on loan approvals and closings!

You should sign and date the original application. Remember that the date the application is submitted and signed triggers the RESPA disclosures, GFE, and TIL, which must be presented to you within three days of the application date.

If the transaction is a purchase and you are currently renting, remember to check into changing your withholding exemptions. Since you will now be able to deduct mortgage interest and property taxes from your taxable income, your tax bill will be lower. Making no changes to withholding will make your refund significantly larger. Check your personnel or human resources department for more information. Or you can go online to www.irs.gov and look at the Employers' Guide to Withholding. This booklet has tables defining the dollar amount of one exemption, given: (1) the amount you are paid; (2) the frequency you get paid; and (3) filing status (single, married filing jointly, etc.). Subtract the amount of interest and property taxes, using your amortization schedule to determine interest paid in the first calendar year, from the adjusted gross income on your previous tax return. Look at the Internal Revenue Service's tax tables to see how much lower your taxes would have been in the previous year with the deductions. The difference in taxes divided by the dollar amount of each exemption, as shown on the Employer's Guide to Withholding, will give you an idea of the number of additional exemptions you should claim. I recommend claiming less than the maximum amount. You will owe penalties and interest if you under-estimate your withholding. You should always check with a tax professional for accurate tax advice.

CHAPTER 8

Understanding the Good Faith Estimate (GFE), the Truth-In-Lending (TIL), and Other Disclosures

The Real Estate Settlement Procedures Act requires that the Good Faith Estimate (GFE) and the Truth-in-Lending (TIL) disclosures, along with a booklet explaining closing costs, be given to you within three days of the date of the original application.

The GFE gives you an idea of what you can expect to pay in closing costs, which are lender fees, attorney fees, recording fees, homeowner's insurance premium, interest from the date of funding through the end of the month, and any additional costs or fees. Sometimes, it is difficult to reflect costs accurately early in the process. Once the credit report is reviewed, it may be necessary to change programs or lenders. However, the initial disclosures should be as accurate and complete as possible. You may request and receive revised disclosures during the process. Once your lender has been selected, your loan approved, and interest rate locked, ask for a revised GFE. Some states require that a revised GFE be given to you if the closing costs exceed a specified percentage of those from the initial disclosure. The settlement statement, a closing document, details every fee and charge. By law, you can request—and receive—the settlement statement twenty-four hours prior to closing. That should give you time to review the closing costs and obtain certified funds for closing.

The TIL disclosure shows what the lender makes in interest rate and fees, along with other information such as late fees and prepayment penalties.

Federal and state laws governing residential real estate transactions are designed to protect you—the client—to ensure that you possess all pertinent information prior to closing and are not blindsided at the closing table.

Good Faith Estimate

Lender fees appear in the first section of the GFE. Those fees which have "PFC" (prepaid finance charge) checked affect the annual percentage rate (APR; explained below). When one is comparing GFEs among lenders, the section on lender fees is crucial. Other fees—attorney, recording, and prepaids—should not vary much from lender to lender, since they are charges from outside entities.

Prepaids, or items required to be paid in advance, include interest, homeowner's insurance, and mortgage insurance. During the initial interview, enough information to provide accurate amounts of these items will probably not be available. On purchases, prepaids are usually part of closing costs that the buyer brings to closing out of pocket, even if the seller is paying closing costs.

Prepaid interest is collected from the date of funding through the end of the calendar month. A purchase transaction funds the date of closing, as do refinances of investment property. A refinance of a primary residence or second home funds after the three-day right of rescission; if the closing package is signed on Monday, you have until midnight Thursday to cancel the transaction. The loan will fund on Friday. Saturdays are counted as a rescission day but not a funding day. Sundays and holidays are not counted as either a rescission or funding day. If a closing package for a primary residence refinance is signed on a Thursday, the rescission days are Friday, Saturday, and Monday. The loan will fund on Tuesday. *There is no rescission period for refinancing an investment property.*

GOOD FAITH ESTIMATE

Lender:	Sales Price:
Address:	Base Loan Amount:
	Total Loan Amount:
Applicant(s):	Interest Rate:
	Type of Loan:
Property Address:	Preparation Date:
	Loan Number:

The information provided below reflects estimates of the charges which you are likely to incur at the settlement of your loan. The fees listed are estimates - actual charges may be more or less. Your transaction may not involve a fee for every item listed.
The numbers listed beside the estimates generally correspond to the numbered lines contained in the HUD-1 or HUD-1A settlement statement which you will be receiving at settlement. The HUD-1 or HUD-1A settlement statement will show you the actual cost for items paid at settlement.

800	ITEMS PAYABLE IN CONNECTION WITH LOAN:		1100	TITLE CHARGES:	
801	Origination Fee @ % + $	$	1101	Closing or Escrow Fee	$
802	Discount Fee @ % + $	$	1102	Abstract or Title Search	$
803	Appraisal Fee	$	1103	Title Examination	$
804	Credit Report	$	1105	Document Preparation Fee	$
805	Lender's Inspection Fee	$	1106	Notary Fee	$
806	Mortgage Insurance Application Fee	$	1107	Attorney's Fee	$
807	Assumption Fee	$	1108	Title Insurance	$
808	Mortgage Broker Fee	$			$
810	Tax Related Service Fee	$			$
811	Application Fee	$			$
812	Commitment Fee	$			$
813	Lender's Rate Lock-In Fee	$			$
814	Processing Fee	$			$
815	Underwriting Fee	$	1200	GOVERNMENT RECORDING AND TRANSFER CHARGES:	
816	Wire Transfer Fee	$	1201	Recording Fee	$
			1202	City/County Tax/Stamps	$
900	ITEMS REQUIRED BY LENDER TO BE PAID IN ADVANCE:		1203	State Tax/Stamps	$
901	Interest for days @ $ /day	$	1204	Intangible Tax	$
902	Mortgage Insurance Premium	$			$
903	Hazard Insurance Premium	$			$
904	County Property Taxes	$			$
905	Flood Insurance	$			$
		$	1300	ADDITIONAL SETTLEMENT CHARGES:	
		$	1301	Survey	$
1000	RESERVES DEPOSITED WITH LENDER:		1302	Pest Inspection	$
1001	Hazard Ins. Mo. @$ Per Mo. $				$
1002	Mortgage Ins. Mo. @$ Per Mo. $				$
1004	Tax & Assmt. Mo. @$ Per Mo. $				$
1006	Flood Insurance	$			$
		$		TOTAL ESTIMATED SETTLEMENT CHARGES:	$
"S"/"B" designates those costs to be paid by Seller/Broker.			"A" designates those costs affecting APR.		

TOTAL ESTIMATED MONTHLY PAYMENT:		TOTAL ESTIMATED FUNDS NEEDED TO CLOSE:	
Principal & Interest	$	Down Payment	$
Real Estate Taxes	$	Estimated Closing Costs	$
Hazard Insurance	$	Estimated Prepaid Items / Reserves	$
Flood Insurance	$	Total Paid Items (Subtract)	$
Mortgage Insurance	$	Other	$
Other	$	CASH FROM BORROWER	$
TOTAL MONTHLY PAYMENT	$		

THIS SECTION IS COMPLETED ONLY IF A PARTICULAR PROVIDER OF SERVICE IS REQUIRED. Listed below are providers of service which we required you to use. The charges indicated in the Good Faith Estimate above are based upon the corresponding charge of the below designated providers.

ITEM NO.	NAME & ADDRESS OF PROVIDER	TELEPHONE NO.	NATURE OF RELATIONSHIP

These estimates are provided pursuant to the Real Estate Settlement Procedures Act of 1974, as amended (RESPA). Additional information can be found in the HUD Special Information Booklet, which is to be provided to you by your mortgage broker or lender, if your application is to purchase residential property and the Lender will take a first lien on the property.

Applicant	Date	Applicant	Date

Applicant	Date	Applicant	Date

☐ This Good Faith Estimate is being provided by a mortgage broker, and no lender has yet been obtained.

The reason interest is collected for the remainder of the month at closing is because mortgage payments are paid in arrears, unlike rent, which is paid in advance. If the purchase loan closes August 25, interest is collected from August 25 through August 31. The first payment is due October 1, which pays the September principal and interest.

Some lenders allow *interest credits*, if the loan closes during the first part of the month (usually by the tenth). If the purchase loan closes August 5, rather than collecting interest from you for the fifth through the thirty-first, the lender credits you with five days of interest on the settlement statement. Then, the first payment would be due September 1, paying the August principal and interest in its entirety. This allows those with limited funds to reduce the money they are required to bring to closing. If you are interested in an interest credit, ask your loan officer if interest credits are allowed, and if so, what day of the month the loan must fund to qualify. Many lenders do not allow interest credits.

Since interest begins accruing on the day the loan funds, using an interest credit does not cost more or less than the traditional method of paying the month's interest at closing. The only difference is when the money is paid: at funding, with the next payment due thirty days from the first of the next month after closing, or the first of the next month. Some buyers have a hard time coming up with funds to close, so interest credits can help a buyer reduce the amount of funds to close.

Homeowner's insurance is a prepaid expense collected at closing. On purchases, the entire annual premium is collected, plus two or three months' premiums for the cushion in the escrow account. For refinances, the amount collected will be a function of how many payments will be made before the premium is due. The difference is collected at closing, plus the cushion. If you are short of funds to close on a purchase, the homeowner's insurance premium may be paid outside of closing (before closing). The insurance agent will send a paid invoice along with the declarations page to the closing attorney/closing agent. An underwriter will not require documentation that funds paid outside closing (POC) are sourced and seasoned.

Title charges are fees from the attorney and/or title company. Keep in mind these fees will change if the closing becomes more complex. Be sure to ask about the charge to close a second mortgage in conjunction with a first mortgage. There will always be a second set of recording fees. Most attorneys and title companies will also charge a fee for closing the second.

Recording fees are fees charged to record the new mortgage and deed on purchases (mortgage only on refinances unless the names on the deed change) at the probate judge's office. Many states also collect tax stamps. Check with your attorney or probate judge's office to find out what fees are collected and how to calculate them. Recording fees are generally calculated based upon the loan amount or number of pages of the documents.

Truth-in-Lending

The truth-in-lending (TIL) disclosure shows you the cost of the loan considering both interest rate and lender fees. The cost is reflected as an annual percentage rate. *Many people confuse the APR with the interest rate on the note. The APR will equal the note rate only when there are no lender fees or in the years after the initial transaction. Your interest rate will be what your loan office has locked and will appear on the note.*

To calculate APR, the interest rate, repayment period, loan amount, and lender fees are required. The lender fees listed on the GFE with "PFC" (prepaid finance charge) marked will be used to calculate the APR. When one is considering several lender programs, given interest rates are the same, the lender with the higher APR has higher closing costs.

A confusing aspect of the truth-in-lending disclosure is that the amount financed is less than the loan amount. The difference is the lender fees. The rationale is if a lender gives you "X" amount of money on a loan, and you give them "Y" amount in closing costs, you really only received the money listed in the amount financed block. This notice is for disclosure purposes only. The loan amount will be the amount on the application, approval, and note.

Demand feature. Most notes include a demand feature, which "demands" that the entire remaining balance on the loan be paid in full if payments have not been made on time. This feature is part of the foreclosure procedure. If the loan is in default and is not paid in full within a specified period, the lender will foreclose on the property. If the loan is paid as scheduled, the demand feature cannot be exercised.

Late charge. Usually 5 percent of the payment amount is charged if the loan payment is more than fifteen days late. Incurring a late charge will not necessarily adversely affect your credit rating on the credit report. The late charge applies if the payment is more than fifteen days late. A late payment is reported on the credit report if the payment is more than thirty days late.

Ask your loan officer if there is a prepayment penalty on your loan program. *Note: New mortgage industry regulations have disallowed prepayment penalties.*

Most programs do not allow a refund of the finance charge (interest) if the loan is paid off early. This is because most programs have payments that pay interest that has already accrued in the past. Interest is not collected in advance. Remember, the first due date after closing pays the previous month's principal and interest.

Most programs do not allow a new buyer to assume an existing loan from the current owner.

If you bought your home on a Veterans Administration loan program, a buyer can assume your loan given the buyer has appropriate qualifications: credit, income, and debt ratio within the guidelines. The veteran will assume your loan using his VA eligibility and yours will be free for you to use again. If the buyer is not a qualified veteran, with a VA certificate of eligibility, the only way he can assume your loan is if you let him use your certificate of eligibility. This is a very bad idea. ***Do not let a buyer***

TRUTH-IN-LENDING DISCLOSURE STATEMENT
(THIS IS NEITHER A CONTRACT NOR A COMMITMENT TO LEND)

Applicants: Prepared By:

Property Address:

Application No: Date Prepared:

ANNUAL PERCENTAGE RATE	FINANCE CHARGE	AMOUNT FINANCED	TOTAL OF PAYMENTS
The cost of your credit as a yearly rate	The dollar amount the credit will cost you	The amount of credit provided to you or on your behalf	The amount you will have paid after making all payments as scheduled
%	$	$	$

☐ REQUIRED DEPOSIT: The annual percentage rate does not take into account your required deposit
PAYMENTS: Your payment schedule will be:

Number of Payments	Amount of Payments **	When Payments Are Due	Number of Payments	Amount of Payments **	When Payments Are Due	Number of Payments	Amount of Payments **	When Payments Are Due
		Monthly Beginning:			Monthly Beginning:			Monthly Beginning:

☐ DEMAND FEATURE: This obligation has a demand feature.
☐ VARIABLE RATE FEATURE: This loan contains a variable rate feature. A variable rate disclosure has been provided earlier.

CREDIT LIFE/CREDIT DISABILITY: Credit life insurance and credit disability insurance are not required to obtain credit, and will not be provided unless you sign and agree to pay the additional cost

Type	Premium	Signature
Credit Life		I want credit life insurance. Signature:
Credit Disability		I want credit disability insurance. Signature:
Credit Life and Disability		I want credit life and disability insurance. Signature:

INSURANCE: The following insurance is required to obtain credit:
☐ Credit life insurance ☐ Credit disability ☐ Property insurance   ☐ Flood insurance
You may obtain the insurance from anyone you want that is acceptable to creditor
☐ If you purchase ☐ property ☐ flood insurance from creditor you will pay $ for a one year term.
SECURITY: You are giving a security interest in:
☐ The goods or property being purchased   ☐ Real property you already own.
FILING FEES: $
LATE CHARGE: If a payment is more than   days late, you will be charged   % of the payment
PREPAYMENT: If you pay off early, you
☐ may   ☐ will not   have to pay a penalty.
☐ may   ☐ will not   be entitled to a refund of part of the finance charge.
ASSUMPTION: Someone buying your property
☐ may   ☐ may, subject to conditions   ☐ may not   assume the remainder of your loan on the original terms.
See your contract documents for any additional information about nonpayment, default, any required repayment in full before the scheduled date and prepayment refunds and penalties
☐ * means an estimate   ☐ all dates and numerical disclosures except the late payment disclosures are estimates.

* * NOTE: The Payments shown above include reserve deposits for Mortgage Insurance (if applicable), but exclude Property Taxes and Insurance.

THE UNDERSIGNED ACKNOWLEDGES RECEIVING A COMPLETED COPY OF THIS DISCLOSURE.

_____   _____
(Applicant)   (Date)   (Applicant)   (Date)

_____   _____
(Applicant)   (Date)   (Applicant)   (Date)

_____

use your VA eligibility to assume your VA loan. If your VA eligibility is on the loan, *you* are still responsible. Any late payments or defaults made on this loan will be reflected on your credit report.

I know of instances where nonveterans assumed Veterans Administration loans using the seller's VA eligibility, defaulted on the loan, and the foreclosure was reported on the veteran's credit report.

Other Disclosures

There are many other disclosures required to be given to you, with a signed copy in your application package. Many are standard, such as an authorization to obtain a credit report, and verifications of deposit, employment, and other information. *Other disclosures are required by various states and lenders.*

Following are the basic disclosures:

- Information booklet explaining closing costs. (*Must be given to you within three days of the original application on purchase transactions, per RESPA.*)

- Authorization by you for the lender to obtain information, including ordering a credit report, documenting assets and liabilities, and verifying rent or mortgage payments.

- Privacy policy.

- Client (you) may select the attorney/title company and appraiser as long as the lender approves.

- Broker agreement, which discloses broker charges and fees and states that the client is under no obligation to close the loan with the broker.

- Disclosure of any business relationships the lender has with a third party in this transaction. (For example, the lender has an ownership or other financial interest in the appraisal or credit report company.)

- Servicing disclosure. States the lender has the right to sell the loan and discloses the percentage of loans sold in the past.

- The right of the client to receive a copy of the appraisal. (*Always* ask for the appraisal to be e-mailed to you!)

- Flood zone notification. If the property is in a flood zone, the client must obtain flood insurance. (See Chapter 15, "The Appraisal, Title Work, and Homeowner's Insurance.")

- Equal credit opportunity. No discrimination in making loans

- Federal fair lending notice. No discrimination based upon race, color, religion, sex, marital status, national origin, or ancestry.

- Up-front fees may be charged (credit report and appraisal).

- Consumer handbook on adjustable rate mortgages (if applicable) have been given to you.

CHAPTER 9

SELECTING THE LOAN PROGRAM

When one is selecting a loan program, the following are considered:

- Credit score

- Down payment availability (for purchases)

- Ability to document income

- Assets

- Debt ratio

- Length of time you plan to be in the property (If you are planning to sell within three to five years, an adjustable rate fixed for five or seven years may be appropriate, if the initial interest rate is significantly lower than current fixed rates.)

- Primary residence or investment (cash flow and property management issues)

- Payment affordability. Shorter repayment periods have lower interest rates, but the payments will be higher given the shorter repayment period. If the property is an investment, consider your ability to make payments if the property is not rented and generating income.

Your loan officer can help you decide the program that is best for you.

Basic Program Requirements

Basic programs under Fannie Mae or Freddie Mac guidelines should have the same general guidelines regardless of the lender.

Full income/asset documentation. These loan programs have the lowest interest rates, may be fixed or adjustable interest rates, and have varying repayment periods. Both income and assets must be fully documented. Income documentation requirements stipulate two years' history with a verification of employment or W2s and latest pay stubs. Prior to releasing the closing package, many lenders perform a verbal verification of employment to ensure you are still employed.

Stated income (documented assets). This program is no longer available. Information is provided on the program in case it is ever reinstated. Income is listed on the application but not documented. As long as the income is reasonable given the job, the underwriter will not question it. Since assets are documented, make sure any bank statements or other assets used do not show income, including direct deposit of pay. If so, mark out the dollar amount. Documenting income—*having income show up on **any** bank statement or tax return, even inadvertently, on a stated income program is grounds for the loan to be declined.* Employment is verified.

*Remember, stated income programs **were not** designed to get you approved for a loan you cannot afford. The stated income programs recognize that some income, especially in the case of a self-employed person, cannot be documented under Fannie Mae/Freddie Mac guidelines. On these programs, actual income can be counted; just do not make up income that does not exist! That is fraud!*

Misuse of this program contributed to the mortgage crises and caused it to be discontinued.

The information on stated income programs is provided for when and if they are reinstated.

<u>Stated income/stated assets</u> (SISA). Income and assets are stated on the application but not verified. Employment is verified. These programs have higher interest rates. Note: Fannie Mae and Freddie Mac no longer purchase SISA loans.

<u>Self-employed.</u> To qualify as self-employed, regardless of income documentation, you must document that you have been self-employed for at least two years. Acceptable documentation includes:

- Two years' business license

- Two years' professional license

- Two years' Schedule C from IRS form 1040 (*Remember, if you are on a stated income program, mark out all income and expenses before submission!*)

- Two years' Schedule K from IRS form 1040

<u>Interest only.</u> These programs allow you to pay interest only, no principal, for a specified period. After the initial interest-only period, the payment will be fully amortized with principal and interest payments due. Although the payment will be somewhat lower than a fully amortized principal and interest payment, the amount of a fully amortized payment applied to principal is small during the early years of the program. There will not be a huge reduction in the payment amount for the interest-only programs.

<u>Balloon mortgage.</u> A mortgage with periodic installments of principal and interest, with payments for a specified period of time, after which the remaining balance is due. (Example: 30/15 mortgages are amortized over thirty years with the remaining balance due at the end of fifteen years.)

<u>Pay option.</u> The misuse of this program was a contributor to the mortgage crises. The program was designed specifically for those with income that varies throughout the year or seasonal investment property income. If you own a condominium in a ski resort that you rent to others during the ski season, you may not have income during the "off" season, causing cash flow problems. Each month you are offered four payment options: (1) fully amortized thirty-year principal and interest payment, (2) fully amortized fifteen-year principal and interest payment, (3) interest-only payment, and (4) a minimum payment similar to the minimum payment due on a credit card. The theory behind these options is that you pay fully amortized payments during the months your income is high, or your investment property is fully rented, but have smaller payments during the periods of lower income or empty investment property.

The problem with this program arises if you always pay only the minimum payment due, which will lead to negative amortization (owing more than the value of the property). With each minimum payment, the principal is not reduced *and* the interest accrued may not be fully paid. The unpaid interest is added to the principal balance. Over a period of time, you could put yourself in a position of negative amortization, or negative equity, especially in a declining real estate market. Although these programs are recast (reevaluated) every few years, there is still a potential for you to be in a position of negative amortization. Another problem with this program is the interest rate. The initial rate was extremely low—under 2 percent—for some introductory period, but would adjust at scheduled intervals. The interest-only payments would get higher and higher. I did not offer these programs unless someone specifically asked for them. I was always able to talk the client out of the pay option program and never closed one.

Unfortunately, the program was misused. Instead of using the programs to help those with irregular cash flow, they were used to approve clients for loan amounts much higher than they could otherwise afford. The loan was supposed to be approved at a higher qualifying rate. As rates adjusted upward, homeowners could not afford any payment other than the minimum payment. As unpaid interest was rolled into the loan and the real estate market slowed, people found they owed more on the home than they could afford. Negative equity prevented them from refinancing.

<u>VA.</u> Lenders to qualified veterans are guaranteed repayment by the Veterans Administration. You must qualify on credit, debt ratio, and income for lender programs. No down payment is required. You must have an eligibility certificate—either your own or the certificate of the person whose loan you are assuming.

<u>FHA.</u> Loans that are guaranteed by the Federal Housing Administration. The FHA programs are primarily for those with low to moderate income or first-time homebuyers with little credit history and a small down payment amount.

Down Payment

The lowest-rate programs usually require a down payment of a minimum of 5 percent of the sales price for primary residences or second homes. Investment properties require a 10 percent down payment. The funds have to be sourced (documented that the money is from an approved source) and seasoned (in your account for at least sixty days). If the money has been your account for sixty days, the money is considered to be sourced and seasoned. Any large deposits must be documented (sourced).

Tax refunds are considered sourced and seasoned.

Equity from the sale of the current residence is a valid source of funds for the down payment and closing costs of this transaction. The settlement statement from the sale of the current residence will be required to document the amount of money you receive.

Gifts from immediate family members are possible on most programs. The 3-percent-down programs allow the entire 3 percent down payment to be a gift. On the conforming programs, you may use a gift for a down payment, but you must have 5 percent of your own funds in the transaction. An exception is: when the gift is at least 20 percent of the sales price, you are not required to have your own funds in the transaction. Documentation required when monetary gifts are used as a down payment includes a gift letter, stating your relationship and the fact that the money is a gift and does not need to be repaid. Sometimes asset documentation showing the relative had the money to give will be required.

Borrowing from your 401(k) is an acceptable source of your down payment and funds to close. If you are borrowing from your 401(k), you must document the payment and terms of the loan, which will be listed on your application as a liability and counted on your debt ratio. These loans usually take at least thirty days, so make sure you tell your loan officer and Realtor, because this may affect how quickly you can close.

Veterans Administration loans have relatively low rates and do not require a down payment. Other no-down-payment programs, if available, generally have higher rates than those requiring a down payment.

Reducing the Amount of Funds to Close

Most programs require that the funds to close be sourced and seasoned (generally, the money must be in your account for sixty days, hence the requirement for two months' statements on the accounts).

If you are having a hard time coming up with sourced and seasoned funds to close a purchase, you should consider paying the first year's homeowner's insurance premium directly to the agent. The agent will send the insurance declarations page, along with the paid invoice, to the processor and the attorney. The settlement statement will show the premium as a POC item and will generally not require further documentation.

Earnest money, or "consideration" given when the contract is signed, is not usually sourced or seasoned. A larger earnest money payment means less money you must bring to closing. The amount of earnest money paid must be documented, either by front and back copies of the cancelled check or a statement on the Realtor's letterhead that the money was received, if the amount is greater than 2 percent of the sales price. Earnest money paid is generally not documented when it is less than 2 percent of the sales price. Of course, the underwriter may ask for documentation of the earnest money regardless of the amount as a condition for closing.

Closing at the end of the month will save several hundred dollars in prepaid interest.

If you must close at the beginning of the month, find out if the lender allows interest credits. Many do not. This will eliminate the prepaid interest you must pay at closing. If interest credits are allowed, loans must fund by a certain date—usually the tenth of the month. Rather than collecting interest from the date of closing through the end of the month, the lender credits you for the interest from the first of the month through the closing/funding date. The first payment is due on the first of the next month, paying the entire interest due on the previous month. For example, if the purchase loan closes August 5, rather than collecting interest from the client for the fifth through the thirty-first, the lender credits you five days of interest on the settlement statements. Then, the first payment would be due on September 1, paying August principal and interest in its entirety.

Purchasing a Property Owned by a Relative

When a relative owns the property that you want to buy, the relative may give you a gift of equity—the difference between the sales price and the appraised value, to be used instead of a down payment. No cash is involved in the gift of equity, and the transaction is treated similarly to a rate/term refinance. The loan-to-value is based on the appraised value rather than the sales price. The relative must submit a letter stating the nature of their relationship to you and that the equity is a gift with no repayment required. Most programs require you to have at least 5 percent of your own funds in the transaction unless the gift of equity is 20 percent or more of the sales price.

An alternative to a purchase with a gift of equity is adding you to the deed, and then you refinance on a cash-out transaction, paying the relative the amount of money required. The advantages of this are being able to use the property's equity, no down payment (usually), and the ability to roll in closing costs. There will be attorney and recording fees to add you to the deed, but those will probably be offset by the cost savings of refinancing rather than purchasing. There will be a three-day right of rescission if you will be living in the property.

Some loan programs have no "seasoning" requirements; once the deed is recorded, you can proceed with the cash-out refinance. Other lenders require a period before you are allowed to refinance after being added to the deed. Check the lender and loan program for seasoning requirements.

Bridge Loans

Those who want to purchase a new home before they sell their former home frequently ask about bridge loans. These programs have higher interest rates and are only necessary in extreme circumstances (high debt ratio, must move and purchase immediately). A bridge loan allows you to pull the equity out of your existing home for the down payment on the new home, with only one mortgage payment for the next six months.

The bridge loan refinances the current home's mortgage(s) plus cash out for the down payment on the new home. Interest is prepaid for six months at funding, so no payments will be due for six months. You take enough cash out for the down payment on your new home. (*Note: The cash out **must** be used as a down payment on the new home.*) The bridge loan lender finances the new home. You must make regular payments on the loan for the new home. You have six months to sell your current home and pay off the bridge loan. If the home has not sold in six months, you pay interest-only payments for the next six months. Most bridge loans must be paid off within twelve months. Rates and fees on both loans—the refinance of the current home and the financing for the new home—are generally higher than could be found otherwise.

An Alternative to Bridge Loans

The equity in the current home is an acceptable down payment source for the new home financing. A home equity line of credit on the existing residence is a quick and easy way to pull the equity out of the current home and qualify for the lowest-rate programs with 5 percent down on the purchase of the new home. Many HELOCs have no closing costs. Most require that the loan be open for two or three years or closing costs (usually only a few hundred dollars) must be repaid. However, some lenders will waive closing costs if the HELOC is closed due to the sale of the subject property. They will also generally waive the closing costs if a HELOC is opened on the new home, perhaps to avoid private mortgage insurance by keeping the first mortgage at 80 percent of the purchase price.

Local banks sometimes have good rates and terms for second mortgage home equity lines of credit and can usually close the loans within a few days. Check with several second mortgage lenders, or ask your mortgage broker, to compare rates and terms.

If you are using a HELOC on the current home as the source of the down payment, remember that the payment will be added to the debt ratio, along with the existing first mortgage payment on the current residence when the new home loan is being approved. Also, provide the documentation on the rate, terms, and payments in your application package for the underwriter to review. Underwriters will usually require a copy of the note and the mortgage as documentation.

CHAPTER 10

LOAN APPROVAL

Applications can either be uploaded directly, or manually entered into the lender's Web site for approval. Approvals should be available within a few minutes of submission and will usually include your credit report. You will be asked to provide some income documentation—usually your latest pay stub—because the initial approval will be based upon your income, debt ratio, and credit score.

Once your loan is approved, your loan officer should be able to issue you an approval letter, which will probably contain a statement indicating that the loan approval is subject to no changes in your income, debt, or credit rating, and the appraised value of the property. Once your loan is approved, be sure you do not increase your debt or lower your income without informing your loan officer. Any changes in your financial situation could affect your loan approval. Be sure to pay all your bills on time to keep your credit score high. I had clients that quit their jobs or filed bankruptcy after I had approved their loans and before they found a house, which resulted in the loan ultimately being declined.

Your lender will give you a generic approval letter prior to your searching for a home that states how much you can borrow to assure the seller's Realtor you can obtain financing. These letters should state the amount for which you will qualify. Your Realtor should keep this letter confidential.

Most contracts require that you obtain a loan approval within a specified number of days. For contract-required approval letters, I recommend that a dollar amount is *not* included in the approval letter, because that can affect the price negotiations. Normally, we would tell the Realtor the price range for which the client could be approved. Once a property was found, we would issue a letter to be released to the listing agent saying that the client had been approved to purchase the property at a specific address. This keeps your financial situation private. Sellers and Realtors do not need to know the terms of your loan and down payment.

CHAPTER 11

LOCKING AN INTEREST RATE

You should be able to lock the loan once it is approved in the lender's system.

Lenders have different policies on locking loans, but no lender wants locked loans that do not fund. Some lenders will penalize brokers if they lock too many loans that never fund. Sometimes, people apply with several brokers/lenders, locking whenever/wherever they can. I would not lock a loan for a client until I was relatively sure he was not still shopping around. Sometimes this cost me the deal, but I found those clients who were not loyal were just as likely to pull the loan at the end to go with someone else, wasting all the time, effort, and expense I had put into the file. Ask lenders what their locking policy is.

Pricing a Rate

Lenders post rates and prices (points) associated with the rate and length of the lock period to brokers and loan officers. A base rate, or "par" rate, has no points or cost. Points, associated with various rates and lock periods, are expressed in either eighths or tenths of a percent. One point is 1 percent of the loan amount.

Lenders usually charge fractions of points, or "add-ons," for different situations, including smaller loan amounts, cash-out refinances, not collecting escrows, existing or new second mortgages, investment property, and extended lock periods. Add-ons are usually priced at a quarter to one and a half or two points (one and a half or two points for investment property) and will vary among lenders. Depending upon the market, which fluctuates, the add-ons may increase the rate itself.

When pricing a loan, a loan officer will determine the total "add-ons" and quote a rate based on the lender's current pricing. For example, if you had a cash-out refinance on your primary residence which cost half a point (0.5) and you did not want to escrow for taxes and insurance which cost a quarter of a point (0.25), your total cost would be 0.75 points. From the chart below, you can see that for a thirty-day lock your best rate, without having to pay anything, is 6 percent. Six percent is priced at minus 0.75 points, which will absorb the add-ons. A loan requiring no add-ons locked for thirty days could receive an interest rate of 5.625 percent.

If you could lock at 5.625 percent but wanted to buy your rate down to 5.5 percent, it would cost you 1.75 percent of the loan amount, or $1750 on a $100,000 loan. Points are fees that the lender receives, which affect the annual percentage rate. Points charged may be rolled into the loan amount on refinances. On purchases, either the buyer or seller, depending upon the terms of the contract, must pay the cost of the points at closing.

Thirty days is usually a long enough lock period to be sure your loan closes and funds. Be sure to discuss any unusual circumstances that may delay closing with your loan officer or processor.

Points expressed in eighths of a point				
Conventional Conforming Thirty-Year Fixed				
	Price			
Rate	15-Day	30-Day	45-Day	60-Day
5.500%	1.625%	1.750%	1.875%	2.000%
5.625%	-0.25%	-0.125%	0.000%	0.125%
5.750%	-0.500%	-0.375%	-0.250%	-0.125%
5.875%	-0.750%	-0.625%	-0.500%	-0.375%
6.000%	-0.875%	-0.750%	-0.625%	-0.500%
6.125%	-1.500%	-1.375%	-1.250%	-1.125%
6.250%	-2.000%	-1.875%	-1.750%	-1.625%
6.375%	-2.250%	-2.125%	-2.000%	-1.875%
6.500%	-2.750%	-2.625%	-2.500%	-2.375%
6.625%	-3.250%	-3.125%	-3.000%	-2.875%
6.750%	-3.750%	-3.625%	-3.500%	-3.375%

Free Rate Float Downs

Some lenders will advertise free rate float downs if the rate drops after you lock your loan. My experience has been that those loans are locked higher than the market rate in order to absorb the cost of lowering the rate if the rate goes down. Lenders are not in the business of losing money. If you are considering a program that offers a free float down, check other rates and programs to determine if you are being offered a competitive rate initially. I never offered these programs to my clients, because I did not think they were necessary. The market usually does not have wild fluctuations (although it can and has!). The rate should not vary a great deal from the time a loan is locked until it closes and funds. An eighth or quarter of a point will not make a drastic difference in payments on most loans. Chasing the absolutely lowest rate is futile and stressful. When it comes time to lock your loan, determine if the rate you are quoted is satisfactory, then lock the loan and stop following the rates!

Yield Spread

Yield spread, or the amount of money paid "on the back" above the par rate is a sensitive issue in the mortgage industry. Yield spread is the negative points a rate pays beyond any add-ons to the client. Positive points are costs to the client. Usually, a broker or loan officer is paid the yield spread by the lender, although it can be credited to the client and applied to closing costs. Some brokers have used this as an opportunity to get paid significantly more than the standard 1 percent origination fee and do not always disclose this to the client. Based on the example above, if you had no add-ons you could qualify for a rate of 5.625 percent. If your loan officer locked your loan at 6 percent, he or she would receive 0.75 percent of your loan amount in addition to what other fees he/she charged—$750 on a $100,000 loan. Lender and broker fees must be disclosed. As you can see by the rate charts above, it is difficult, or impossible to hit a par rate on loans most of the time. The yield spread can help offset extra costs and expenses a broker incurs that have not been passed to you. The yield spread can be collected in lieu of an origination fee or in a combination of lower origination fee plus yield spread. The problem with collecting yield spread is not disclosing to the client that it is part of the broker or loan officer's compensation. Most states regulate how much money a mortgage broker can make, usually expressed as a percentage of the loan amount. There is a use to the client for yield spread. When the client cannot pay closing costs and the closing costs cannot be rolled into the loan, yield spread can be used to pay closing costs, usually applied as a broker credit.

When you are locking the interest rate on your loan, you have the right to ask how much, if any, yield spread the rate includes. Your loan officer should be willing to explain any extra add-ons that could affect your rate.

Yield spread will be shown on the settlement statement on page two in the section on lender charges. Since the lender pays yield spread to the broker and it is not an out-of-pocket cost to the buyer or seller, it will be shown in the first column for the description of charges rather than the buyer or seller cost column. The closing attorney or title company employee should indicate any yield spread paid in the discussion of the charges and fees listed on the settlement statement.

CHAPTER 12

YOUR CREDIT

Once the initial approval is obtained through the lender's Web site, your credit report should be available. The report usually includes information from all three bureaus—TransUnion, Equifax, and Experian. The easiest reports to read are the "tri-merged," which list information from all bureaus by credit item. The other report will spit out information by bureau, so you will see the same credit account three times (six times, if there is a co-borrower with the same credit accounts!).

The beginning of the credit report should list public records, which include bankruptcies, tax liens, and judgments. If you have had a bankruptcy, the underwriter will usually require a copy of the complete set of bankruptcy papers. Lenders and programs vary depending upon how far back the bankruptcy was discharged before requiring the papers. Your loan officer will tell you what is required given your loan program.

Each bureau will issue a credit score based upon proprietary formulas considering payment history, amount of debt, how close balances are to card limits, account age, etc. Credit scores range from 300 to 850. Most creditors report to the three major bureaus—Experian, TransUnion, and Equifax. Most lenders use the numerical middle score to evaluate credit. To qualify for the lowest-rate lenders, you should have at least a 680. (Prior to changes in program requirements, the minimum credit score to qualify for the lowest rates was 620–630.) Credit scores of 720 and above will qualify for most any program offered, usually with reduced documentation requirements.

To qualify for a mortgage loan, you should have at least three trade lines opened for a year, with a high balance of at least $1,000.00. Those with no credit history will not qualify for a mortgage loan.

Each trade line will contain information about the account, including type of account (mortgage, installment, or revolving), high balance, current balance, payment history, and if you are the borrower or co-borrower.

If two (or more) unmarried co-borrowers are on the loan, each must have a separate credit report run. Joint reports are for married couples only.

Understanding and Calculating Debt Ratios

A debt ratio is total monthly payments divided by *gross* (before taxes) monthly income. Debts included are mortgage payments, including taxes and insurance; credit card minimum payments; car payments; and other consumer loan payments. For credit cards, the minimum payments due are used to calculate debt ratio, not the amount you actually pay. Utility bills, phone bills, cell phone bills, and insurance payments are not counted in the debt ratio. If they show up on the credit report, they should usually be included in the debt ratio. Most of the lowest-rate programs will allow up to 40 percent debt ratio. Loans may be approved with higher ratios if credit scores are high and/or you have a lot of assets documented. I have seen loans approved with 70 percent to 80 percent debt ratio. An underwriter once told me he had seen a loan approved with a 90 percent debt ratio and many documented assets. Most loans will not be approved with high debt ratios.

Building and Keeping Good Credit

Building good credit is a long-term process that can be destroyed with one bad incident. Your credit history is a record of how you have managed debt and made your payments. A lender will loan you money or issue you credit based upon your history of repaying according to stated terms. Your good credit is a reflection of your character and integrity. Any situations beyond your control that will affect your credit (job loss, illness) should be discussed with your lender as soon as possible.

Debt, which should be strictly managed, should be not used as a way to live beyond your means. Credit cards are a convenient way to make purchases within your budget. *Credit card balances should be paid off monthly.* Carrying balances on credit cards is extremely expensive, especially if you make only the minimum payment each month. Living on credit with high amounts of debt can be devastating if you experience a catastrophic event such as a job loss or major long-term illness that reduces or eliminates income. Wise debt and financial management takes discipline and responsibility. There are many good books and DVDs on the market to help you control and manage your debt.

Your credit score is determined by your credit activity, especially over the past twenty-four months. The farther in the past credit issues are, the less they affect your score. Making payments on time is vital to establishing and maintaining good credit. A payment more than 30 days late will adversely affect your credit score. Most lenders charge a late payment penalty if the payment is ten to fifteen days late, but a late payment should not affect your credit score unless it is more than thirty days late.

Your credit score is also influenced by the number of the number of open, active trade lines and how close the balances are to the limits. If you have $1000 credit card debt, your score will be higher if you have two cards, each with a $1000 limit and a $500 balance, than if you have one card with a $1000 limit and a $1000 balance. This is not to say you should keep multiple credit cards with balances. The point is, you should not keep your credit card balance at the card limit.

Credit from finance companies that traditionally lend to those with lower scores at higher interest rates will have an adverse effect on your credit score.

Divorce decrees sometimes specify which spouse is responsible for certain debt. *Creditors do not recognize divorce decrees to absolve the debt of parties to the loan.* If you signed the note, you are responsible for payment, regardless of what a divorce decree says. I have seen many cases where an individual's credit was ruined because their former spouse was supposed to pay a debt and did not. If you are not responsible for a debt in a divorce, make sure your former spouse is required to refinance the debt out of your name. Follow up to verify that you are no longer responsible for the debt.

If you are selling your home financed with your VA eligibility, *do not* let another person use your eligibility to assume the loan. Although that is a quick and cheap way to sell your home, if the buyer does not have his own VA eligibility to substitute for yours, you could be liable if he stops making the payments. A client came to me to refinance his home. He said he had outstanding credit. His credit report showed a foreclosure. He explained that it was not his—he sold his former residence to someone who assumed his VA loan using his VA eligibility. The buyer ultimately stopped making the mortgage payments. The VA foreclosed on the house; because my client's eligibility was on the loan, his credit was affected just as though he had defaulted. His credit was ruined and he was not able to obtain low-rate loans.

Bankruptcy

Most personal bankruptcies fall into two categories: Chapter 7, which eliminates approved debt; and Chapter 13, which sets a repayment schedule for approved creditors, allowing you to repay pennies on the dollar. A judge will review your bankruptcy petition. Once your bankruptcy papers are filed with the court, your creditors are not allowed to contact you to collect the debt if they have been listed in the bankruptcy. Once the bankruptcy is discharged—within a few weeks for a Chapter 7 or several years for the Chapter 13—you can begin to reestablish your credit.

Mortgage lenders generally want a person to be discharged from the bankruptcy at least four years with reestablished credit before they will consider approving and funding a low-rate loan. I had one lender that would not approve the loan if a bankruptcy had *ever* appeared on the credit report.

Credit Counseling and Credit Repair Programs

Most lenders treat credit counseling programs as bankruptcies. These programs are considered similar to Chapter 13 bankruptcy programs, where the company negotiates a repayment plan with the creditors for the individual to repay the debt for less than owed. The credit report will indicate any liabilities included in a credit counseling program. Underwriting guidelines require individuals to be completely out of the bankruptcy or credit counseling program for a period of time (usually four years) before they can be approved for a loan. People who have been in credit counseling programs have told me the fee some companies charge is several hundred dollars and is charged to their credit card!

Credit repair programs usually dispute the derogatory information and request documentation verifying the payment history and loan authenticity. If you have something on your credit report that is not true or you have a disagreement with the company, you should absolutely dispute the debt. Disputing correct information to have it removed from your credit report is dishonest. The purpose of your credit report is to provide potential lenders a history of how you have paid past debt so they can make a decision to lend you more money. The best way to repair your credit is to work to pay the debt you committed to when you signed the loan papers. Work with your lenders if you are having a problem making payments on time. Most lenders do not want to see you file bankruptcy or stop paying completely. Many will work with you to get your account up to date. As a former collector, I always tried to work with the client as long as they were honest and kept their word. Once they lied about making a payment, I was less likely to make concessions for them. (It can only take so long for a check to make it across town in the mail!) Everyone understands that financial issues happen. The key is to be honest as you work with your creditors to get back on track.

If the person you are dealing with is not helpful, ask to speak with a supervisor. You may have to call back and ask for a supervisor rather than ask the person with whom you have had trouble to transfer you.

CHAPTER 13

VERIFICATIONS

Verification forms may be used in lieu of other documentation from you or the credit report. The verification is sent by the processor to the proper authority for completion. The processor is not allowed to give you verification documentation for completion.

Verification of Deposit (VOD) may be used instead of two months' bank statements. A bank employee completes the form with the current and sixty-day average balances on all accounts.

Verification of Rent or Mortgage (VOR/VOM) may be used if the liability is not reported on the credit report and you do not have cancelled checks to document on-time payments. If the landlord/mortgage holder is an individual, the underwriter may not accept the VOR/VOM. A verification of rent or mortgage from a property management company or lender is acceptable. Most program guidelines do not allow VOR/VOMs from individuals.

Verification of Loan (VOL) is required from a creditor when the debt is not listed on the credit report.

Verification of Employment (VOE) replaces the W2 and pay stub. The VOE provides information on date hired, current wage/salary, overtime, and date of next income review/increase.

The verifications must be completed by the appropriate authority and must list the contact information.

CHAPTER 14

THE REAL ESTATE SALES CONTRACT

The sales contract is a written agreement between the buyer(s) and seller(s) detailing the terms of the sale. One of the documents usually signed at closing is an affidavit stating that the terms of the contract have been completed at closing and there are no other outside agreements. The underwriter will review the terms of the contract in relation to the loan program guidelines.

Buyers' names. List the name(s) on the contract that you plan to use on your application, deed, and mortgage. Many underwriters will require that the names appear exactly as they will be shown on these documents.

Closing costs. Make sure the amount of the seller-paid closing costs is within the program's guidelines. On most Fannie Mae/Freddie Mac programs, the seller may pay up to 3 percent of the sales price in buyer's closing costs and prepaids. *If the property will be non-owner-occupied, the seller contributions to closing costs are limited to 2 percent.*

To apply any of the seller-paid closing costs to prepaids (buyer's interest and homeowner's insurance premium), the contract must state "closing costs and prepaids." Otherwise, the money will be applied to closing costs only. Any leftover amount goes back to the seller.

The seller-paid closing costs are usually built into the price of the house and are subtracted from the proceeds (loan amount plus down payment), with the seller receiving the net amount. Usually the seller will not bring money to the closing (some sellers are unclear about this). If the sales price is not enough to pay off the existing liens, plus closing costs, someone must bring cash to the closing for the closing costs. I always suggested that if the buyer was asking the seller to pay all or part of the closing costs, the dollar amount be listed on the contract. (Example: Seller will pay up to $3,500.00 in closing costs and prepaids.) Stating a limit on the amount the seller will pay helps the seller feel comfortable that he will not be stuck paying an amount higher than expected once he gets to closing.

Closing date. You and the seller will decide how quickly you want to close. Most lenders will tell you it takes at least thirty days to process and close your loan.

Time is of the essence. This harmless-sounding phrase can cause a tremendous amount of stress and threats of lawsuits. "Time is of the essence" is a legal term that refers to the date of closing and possession. If the sale must be closed on or before January 31, and "time is of the essence" is marked "Yes," on February 1, the contract is null and void unless both parties agree to reinstate it. If "time is of the essence" is marked "No" and closing takes place a few days later, most reasonable people would consider the contract still valid. (A closing five or six months later would not be reasonable, of course.)

I had a situation early in my career that emphasized the importance of this little phrase. My client was self-employed and had credit issues. It took longer than usual to get everything processed and approved. The contract said the closing must take place by January 31, and time was of the essence. January 31 was on a Saturday. On Thursday, January 29, we were waiting for the final prior to documents condition—documentation from the IRS that the client had paid overdue taxes (which he finally paid on Thursday, January 29). By the time the IRS faxed the required documentation to me, it was after 6:00 PM. The underwriter could not review the documentation until Friday morning (January 30). By the time the file had received final approval and was ready to close, it was too late to get a package to the attorney by the close of business on Friday (this was before the evolution of e-mailed closing packages; the original had to be sent by overnight delivery to the attorney). We could close Monday, February 2, the next business day. The seller refused and canceled the contract. I suspect he had another buyer willing to pay a higher sales price; otherwise, it did not make any sense to lose the sale. My client was furious and consulted an attorney to sue the seller. The attorney explained that given the "time is of the essence" provision in the contract, the seller was within his rights and it would be futile to sue.

Additional provisions. Many times, the contract includes a provision for the buyer to obtain and accept a home inspection report.

If the additional provisions list personal property that is included in the sale, it *must be removed or listed "at no value."* Some underwriters will require that the reference to "personal property" be removed completely or the file will be underwritten by using a sales price reduced by the value of the personal property. This means you will have to make a larger down payment to make up the difference between the sale price as underwritten and the contract sale price. (Examples of personal property included in the sale are a pool table and equipment, swimming pool equipment, lawn care equipment, other furniture or appliances.) The real estate mortgage lender is financing "real property," so any personal property included in the sale technically reduces the sales price by the value of the personal property.

An appraiser once gave me an easy definition of real versus personal property:

If the item is freestanding or must be unplugged to move, it is personal property. If the item must be unscrewed, it is real property. An exception to this definition is the stove, which usually just plugs in but is usually included in the sale and not questioned.

Allowances. Many times, the contract calls for a carpet allowance or an allowance for repairs or upgrades. An underwriter will disallow these provisions. The work must be completed and paid for at or before closing or the underwritten sales price will be reduced by the amount of the allowance. A lower underwritten sales price will result in a lower loan amount. You will have to bring in a large enough down payment to make the difference in the loan amount and contract sales price. A buyer is not allowed to receive cash at closing from the seller. If repairs or renovations need to be done under the terms of the contract, the appraisal will be done with a value "subject to" the repairs/renovations. The appraiser will have to reinspect and provide a report with pictures of the completed work prior to closing, which results in an additional charge.

"Subject to" work/escrow. Any work required in the contract must be completed prior to closing. Most programs/lenders will not fund the loan while allowing the money to complete the work to be held in an attorney's escrow account. The loan will not be funded until all work is completed. An exception is minor costs of landscaping. If the work is to be done on the structure, it must be completed prior to the closing. The repairs/improvements, or lack of them, affect the value of the house, which is the collateral for the loan. Once the loan has been funded, the lender has no way to verify that the work has been completed and there is no recourse if it has not.

Seller-Generated Contract Forms

Many times, buyers and sellers who are not using a Realtor will generate their own contract from reference books or the Internet. These may be used. If you have a self-generated contract, give it to your loan officer or processor as soon as possible to make sure it meets underwriting guidelines. Review the contract terms to make sure that what the contract states is what you mean to do. I had a closing where both the buyer and seller were extremely upset because what they stated in the contract was not what they meant to do. The attorney explained that everyone was legally bound to conduct the transaction based on the terms of the contract. The only alternative was to cancel the closing and start over with a new contract. They chose to close, but I learned to always let both parties know how the terms they were agreeing to in the contract would affect the closing. If a Realtor is involved, he/she should have a standard contract that he/she will explain to you and the seller.

The Inspection

Although they are not required by the lender, inspections identify problems that may affect the transaction. Even new homes have things wrong with them. Most issues are minor and will be ignored or easily fixed before closing. Some issues, such as structural problems, may be sufficient to cancel the contract. You, the buyer, review the inspection, evaluating the seriousness of each issue. You may ignore the issue, request that the seller repair/replace the item prior to closing, renegotiate the sales price, or cancel the contract and receive a refund of the earnest money.

If you are getting an inspection, do not let your processor order the appraisal until you have a chance to review and accept the inspection report. *Once the appraisal is completed, you owe the fee.* If the transaction is canceled due to the inspection results, you have paid for an appraisal that cannot be used.

Cheryl L. Peck

CHAPTER 15

THE APPRAISAL, TITLE WORK, AND HOMEOWNER'S INSURANCE THE APPRAISAL

The appraisal is a report that compares your house (or the one you are buying) with similar properties close by that have sold recently. The appraiser will visually inspect your property and take measurements. He will find "comparable" sales within a specified distance from your home— usually a mile or less in a suburban area—that have sold within a specified time—usually six to twelve months. To be considered a comparable sale, the property should be similar in size, age, and construction. A distress sale, such as one to avoid foreclosure, will not usually be considered a comparable sale. The appraiser will determine a value for your home based upon the comparison of your subject property with the properties that have sold recently.

Remember, you have a right to receive a copy of your appraisal, so be sure to ask for it! You will probably be asked to pay for the appraisal before the processor orders it.

The appraiser will note any problems he sees with the property that must be corrected prior to closing. A common example is a water stain on the ceiling, which indicates a leak. Although the leak has probably been repaired, the underwriter will probably require a roofer or other professional to inspect the property to ensure that the leak has been fixed, resulting in an additional charge to be paid at closing. The appraisal report should note any problems the appraiser sees, but the inspection is not required and the appraiser usually does not see the report. The appraiser will perform a visual inspection but does not check appliances, water pressure, wiring, plumbing, etc.

The appraiser will note the property zoning and use. He will include pictures of the street around the subject property as well as any other indication that the property is next to property that is zoned commercial. Both Fannie Mae and Freddie Mac have guidelines concerning zoning requirements.

The appraiser will mark the report in either the "as is" or "subject to" box, indicating whether the value depends on future improvements. All "subject to" work must be completed prior to closing. The appraiser must reinspect the property before closing and submit a report with pictures verifying the work has been satisfactorily completed. An additional fee for the final report will usually be charged. A reinspection could delay closing, because the closing package may not be released until all work has been documented as complete.

New construction in new subdivisions can cause a problem if there are no usable comparable sales in the area. A home has to be offered for sale on the open market to be eligible for use as a comparable sale in the appraisal report. Custom home sales contracted between the buyer and the builder cannot be used as comparable sales. New subdivisions of custom homes may not have acceptable comparables within the specified area. Without comparable sales within the distance specified in the underwriting guidelines, the loan may be declined.

The appraisal will note whether the subject property has been listed for sale within the last twelve months. This is done by reviewing multiple listing records, and a property listed for sale by owner will probably not show up. *Remember, if a property has been listed for sale within the last twelve months, Fannie Mae/Freddie Mac guidelines will not allow refinance transactions.*

The appraisal will note whether the property is in a flood zone. If so, you will need to be prepared to obtain flood insurance. The underwriting requirement for flood insurance will come from the flood certification report the closing department orders right before the file is cleared for closing. Those who are refinancing should already know if the property is in a flood zone and requires flood insurance.

Appraisers consider whoever ordered the appraisal to be the client. If your loan officer or processor ordered the appraisal, they have control of it. If you change brokers/lenders, you have to request them to transfer the appraisal to the new lender. Otherwise, the new broker/lender will have to request and pay for a new appraisal.

The appraisal report will probably be e-mailed to the processor. Request that it be e-mailed to you when it is available.

Title Work

The attorney or title company will perform a title search of the courthouse records to ensure all liens and mortgages are paid and released at closing, which allows you to assume ownership of the property with a clear title. Depending upon the attorney's schedule, this could take several days. A title insurance policy will be issued at closing in the lender's name, which is required by the lender. Owner's coverage is optional, and requires a small additional fee; it should be purchased. Title insurance will protect the lender and/or buyer from losses due to title issues that may be discovered after closing. The owner's title policy will protect you for as long as you own the property.

You will receive the title policy by mail about four weeks after the closing. You should keep it in your real estate file. *If you ever refinance, you should take the policy to your mortgage lender to copy and submit to the closing attorney/title company. This will allow the title company to reissue the existing policy, rather than writing a new policy, saving approximately 40 percent on the premium.* (Note: The title insurance premium is a one-time fee paid at closing.)

A survey, which is a drawing of the property showing boundary lines, any improvements, easements, and building setback lines, may be required before title insurance can be issued. The survey will also show any encroachments of structures over any easements or property lines. If the property is in an established subdivision with a lot and block legal description, the survey requirement will usually be waived. A metes and bounds legal description or new construction will usually trigger the requirement for a survey. Surveys are required more often for purchases than refinances. Ask the seller if they have a survey. If not, you may want to get one even if it is not required.

If a married person is to be on the loan and deed alone without the spouse on a primary residence, let your loan officer or processor know, and include your spouse's name. There may be documents a spouse must sign at closing.

The processor will receive the title commitment and the closing protection letter from the title company. The title commitment shows the result of the title search, indicating any liens that must be released prior to closing the current loan in order for title insurance to be issued. The closing protection letter, issued by the attorney's errors and omissions insurance carrier, states that the lender is protected from mistakes made by the attorney.

Note: Remember, a common misconception is that if the seller pays the closing costs, they can select the closing attorney. According to RESPA, the buyer selects the closing attorney subject to the lender's approval. No matter which side of the settlement statement closing costs are listed (buyer's or seller's), the closing costs are built into the sales price. The attorney actually represents the lender (who is funding the loan!) and ensures all documents are correct and complete, and the contract has been fulfilled. The buyer and seller do not usually need separate representation. The majority of the closing package consists of disclosures.

The main documents in the closing package are the settlement statement (listing charges/fees), note (lists terms of loan), and mortgage (puts the lien on the property).

Homeowner's Insurance

On purchases, the first year's homeowner's insurance premium must be paid at closing. On refinances, the amount of the insurance premium collected at closing will depend upon the premium due date (if you are not changing insurance carriers). For refinances, give your loan officer the contact information for your homeowner's insurance agent. For purchases, let your loan officer know your agent's information as soon as you decide whom to use. Most lenders will not allow the closing package to be ordered without prior submission of the insurance declarations page to underwriting.

Refinances

Give your loan officer or processor the insurance declarations page for the property during the initial interview, or at least the name and phone number of your agent. The current "dec" page, which shows the property address, effective dates, and coverage and premium amounts, will be enough to submit the file to underwriting. The processor will notify the insurance agent of the refinance, closing date, new loan number, and mortgagee clause. Some agents require authorization from the client before they will release any information or make changes to the policy. USAA requires client authorization, so if you use USAA insurance be sure to notify them of the refinance, and authorize USAA to talk to your loan officer and processor. USAA issues client ID numbers, so be sure to give yours to your loan officer.

Purchases

You must talk to your insurance agent to determine the specifics of coverage, deductible, and premium. The agent will need a copy of the appraisal, usually by e-mail, and the mortgage information—loan, number, mortgagee clause, and projected closing date. Your processor will see that your agent gets the information he/she needs to provide verification of insurance before closing.

Note: Most lenders will not allow a deductible greater than $1,000.00.

Flood Insurance

If any part of the property is in a flood zone, the entire property is classified as being in a flood zone. If the property is in a flood zone and flood insurance is required, you must obtain an elevation certificate for the structure, developed by reviewing an elevation survey, to determine the flood insurance premium. An elevation survey documents how high above the floodplain the structure sits; the higher the structure is above the floodplain, the lower the flood insurance premium. If the structure is above the floodplain, you can submit the elevation certificate and report to the Federal Emergency Management Agency (FEMA) to have the property ruled out of the flood zone, eliminating the need for flood insurance. This takes about six months, so it is not something that can be done before closing. You would have to obtain the flood insurance, and then cancel it after the ruling is received from FEMA stating the property is outside the flood zone. You should talk to the lender's customer service department after closing to determine the documentation required to change the flood zone classification. You should also keep the elevation certificate and FEMA ruling in your real estate file for use when/if you sell the property.

The elevation survey will cost several hundred dollars. In our area, it ranges between $500 and $600. If you order the survey, you are responsible for paying for it. If the loan does not close for some reason, you still owe for the elevation survey (and appraisal and anything else you have ordered!).

To save time and money, ask the seller if they have a copy of an elevation certificate. If they currently have flood insurance, then they must have had one at some time, although many do not keep up with the documents. The seller's homeowner's insurance agent should have a copy of the elevation certificate if the seller currently has flood insurance. If they are willing to give you a copy, it will save you time and money.

CHAPTER 16

UNDERWRITING

Once the processor has all the documentation and disclosures, he/she will prepare your file for submission to underwriting. The underwriter reviews the application package to verify compliance with lending guidelines and give final approval to the loan. Any required information that was not submitted in the original package will be requested. These requests, called "conditions," must be submitted before the closing package can be ordered. There are two types of conditions: prior to document (PTD) and prior to funding (PTF).

The PTD conditions must be submitted and approved before the closing documents can be ordered and released. An example of a PTD condition is insurance documentation or the seller's signature on the contract. A final approval will not be issued until all PTD conditions have been met. If you have ever gone through the mortgage loan application process, you may remember your loan officer or processor coming back to you for more documentation after you thought everything was completed. Those additional requests were probably the result of conditions issued by the underwriter.

The PTF conditions must be submitted and approved before the loan can fund. An example of a PTF condition is the payoff documentation on an existing mortgage.

CHAPTER 17

THE CLOSING PROCESS

Once all PTD conditions have been cleared, the file will be sent to the lender's closing department and the closing package can be ordered.

Remember, many lenders require the underwriter or closer to perform a verbal verification of employment on all borrowers prior to releasing the closing package. This can hold up the release of the closing package if the contact cannot be reached. Make sure the underwriter has good contact information for a couple of your coworkers.

Closing

You probably will have a projected closing date very early in the process. Keep in close touch with your loan officer and processor to make sure nothing comes up to delay closing. The time it takes to generate and send the closing package will depend upon how many packages were ordered ahead of yours. The last few business days of the month are usually hectic for a lender's closing department. If your package is not ordered soon enough, you may have a problem meeting your schedule.

Ideally, the closing package is ordered early enough to give the attorney/ title company plenty of time to prepare the package, including the settlement statement. By law (RESPA), you can require the settlement statement twenty-four hours prior to closing for review. I always tried to do this (unless we were in the middle of a closing emergency!) because it eliminates stress at the closing table. Prior review of the settlement statement by all involved parties also saves time, because you can ask questions and correct errors prior to closing.

Reviewing the settlement statement the day before closing will let you know how much money you are required to bring to the closing early enough to avoid a last-minute rush to the bank. *Funds to close must be certified funds—no personal checks are accepted.* Some banks and credit unions, which charge a fee for a bank check, will waive the fee if the purpose of the check is a real estate closing transaction. Be sure to ask the teller!

The closing packages are electronically transmitted, so it is easy to send you a copy. You probably will not care about reviewing the entire package, just the settlement statement and the note. The closing secretary at the attorney's office/title company can send copies to all involved parties.

I strongly recommend you ask for a copy of the settlement statement and note the day before closing.

Some people insist on reading every page of the closing package. To avoid wasting everyone's time at the closing table, ask for a copy of the closing package at least twenty-four hours prior to closing.

The attorney or title representative will explain the documents in the closing package to the client(s). The main documents to consider are:

1. **Settlement statement**, which lists all the charges and fees involved in the transaction and who pays and receives what; lists all credits (earnest money, items paid outside of closing); and lists final totals on funds required from/to the borrower/buyer and seller.

2. **Note**, which details the terms and conditions of the loan, including loan amount, interest rate, fixed versus adjustable rate, repayment period, and prepayment penalty, if any.

3. **Mortgage**, which places a lien on the property equal to the loan amount.

These documents are standard forms. Check the note to make sure the loan amount, interest rate, and terms are what you expected. Check the mortgage to verify your name and property address are correct.

The other documents in the closing package are mostly disclosures and affidavits (you intend to live in the property, all terms of the contract have been fulfilled with this closing, you will cooperate in correcting errors found after closing, etc.).

I heard many horror stories over the years about clients who got to closing and found the rate and terms of the loan were not what they were promised. Usually, the interest rates were higher, sometimes by several points! (This is a good reason to require the settlement statement and note twenty-four hours before closing!) If that happens to you, *do not close!* On purchases, you will be under a lot of pressure to close—everyone has movers scheduled, the sellers need their money, Realtors and loan officers want to get paid—but do not sign any documents that do not match what you were told about the terms of the loan. Closing packages can be redone. Do not commit yourself to a loan that does not match what you were originally told. If you are refinancing, you have three days to consider the transaction and cancel if you change your mind.

On a purchase, you will receive a copy of the unrecorded deed in the closing package. The deed is the title to the property, showing ownership. Unlike car titles, which are retained by the lender until the loan is paid, the original deed will be sent to you once it is recorded. Many states have a homestead exemption on property taxes that saves you money on your property taxes if you live in the house.

Cheryl L. Peck

Remember:

Ask for the settlement statement and note a day before closing.

Your funds to close must be certified funds.

If the deal was not what you were promised, walk away!

CHAPTER 18

AFTER THE CLOSING

You will you receive your recorded (original) deed about four to six weeks after you close the purchase of your home. If your state and county offer a homestead exemption for property taxes on primary residences, you must take the recorded deed to the tax assessor's office and claim your homestead exemption. Your property taxes could drop as much as 50 percent! You will also receive your title insurance policy if the transaction was a purchase and you purchased the owner's title policy.

Save Thousands of Dollars in Interest

Ask your loan officer to give you an amortization schedule which breaks down how much of your payment is going to reduce the principal balance and how much is going to interest each month for the life of the loan. There are also Web sites that will allow you to generate an amortization schedule given loan amount, interest rate, and repayment period.

An easy way to save tens of thousands of dollars in interest during the life of your loan is to pay extra principal payments each month. You must make a payment every month, unlike for some consumer loans you cannot pay ahead.

The amortization schedule below is based upon a loan amount of $250,000 for thirty years at a 6.5 percent fixed interest rate. The principal and interest payment is $1580.17. (Taxes and insurance will usually be added but do not affect this exercise.)

Notice that each month, the amount of the payment going to principal slowly increases and the amount going to interest slowly decreases as you pay the principal balance lower.

The first month, you make your regular payment plus the principal payment of $227.23 listed for month two. You have just saved month two's interest of $1352.94!

The second month, you make a regular payment; however, you are on month three of the schedule. You add the principal payment for month four of $229.70 to your payment. You save month four's interest of $1350.47. In two months, you have saved $2703.41 in interest. The third month, you will be on payment five of the schedule. You can see how quickly your interest savings add up when you make the extra principal payment!

Pmt	Principal	Interest	Prin Bal
1	226.00	1354.17	249774.00
2	227.23	1352.94	249546.77
3	228.46	1351.71	249318.31
4	229.70	1350.47	249088.61
5	230.94	1349.23	248857.67
6	232.19	1347.98	248625.48
7	233.45	1346.72	248392.03
8	234.71	1345.46	248157.32
9	235.98	1344.19	247921.34
10	237.26	1342.91	247684.08
11	238.55	1341.62	247445.53
12	239.84	1340.33	247205.69

You can pay as many extra principal payments as you want each month. When the principal payments become too large to make an additional principal payment, you can pay any amount you want. *Be sure to note on your payment coupon that the extra payment amount should be applied to the principal balance!* Otherwise, the mortgage company will not know how to post the additional money sent. Of course, you can make an additional principal payment of any amount at any time, but using the amortization schedule lets you keep up with how much interest you have saved! It does not take long for the savings to add up!

GLOSSARY

Adjustable rate mortgage (ARM): A mortgage loan in which the interest rate may change at specified periods of time by a predetermined margin according to a preselected index.

Amortization: Gradual debt reduction, based upon installment payments according to the original loan amount, interest rate, and repayment period.

Amortization schedule: Identifies the amount of principal and interest paid for each payment during the life of the loan.

Annual percentage rate (APR): Discloses yield to the lender. APR is the amount, expressed as a percentage of the loan amount that the lender receives, including interest payments and lender fees.

Appraisal: A report by a licensed appraiser, which evaluates the subject property with recent sales of similar properties in the area to determine the value of the subject property.

Appreciation: The increase in a property's value due to improvements and/or current market conditions.

Balloon mortgage: A mortgage with periodic installments of principal and interest payments for a specified period of time, after which the remaining balance is due. (Example: 30/15 mortgages are amortized over thirty years with the remaining balance due at the end of fifteen years.)

Balloon payment: The lump sum payment due at the end of the specified period to pay off the mortgage.

Basis point: One percent of the loan amount; used when quoting yield spread or points paid for the interest rate.

Cap: The maximum amount an adjustable rate mortgage can change at each adjustment period and the life of the loan.

Closing: Finalizing the sales or refinance transaction, including signing the mortgage loan closing package, transferring title to the property from the seller to the buyer (if applicable), and paying all fees.

Closing costs: Fees incurred to finalize the transaction, including lender fees, attorney/title company fees, recording fees, and prepaid interest and insurance.

Closing protection letter (CPL): A letter from the attorney's errors and omissions insurance company stating that the lender is protected from attorney mistakes.

Collateral: Security for a debt. A mortgage places a lien on the subject property as collateral for the loan.

Credit score: A numerical value given to assess the credit/payment history of an individual. The higher the score, the better the credit. Most programs with relatively low rates require scores in the 700s. Three bureaus report credit scores. Most loan programs use the middle of the three scores for underwriting purposes.

Deed: A legal document showing ownership of real property conveyed by the seller to the buyer. The original recorded deed is held by the owner of the property. It is *not* like a car title held by the lender until the mortgage is paid.

Down payment: Money paid at closing toward the purchase price of the home. The lowest-rate programs require 5 percent of the sales price as a down payment.

Equity: The difference between the fair market value and the mortgage loan amount(s), representing an asset of the owner.

Escrow account: An account set up by the lender to hold monthly payments of real estate taxes and homeowner's insurance premium payments. The lender pays taxes and insurance from this account when due.

Escrow payment: The amount of the total monthly mortgage payment (PITI) that is for taxes and insurance (TI).

Fair market value: The amount a seller can reasonably expect to sell the property for in an open market.

Fannie Mae: A shareholder-owned company with a federal charter to buy real estate mortgage loans from banks and lenders to maximize the availability of mortgage funds to homeowners. The mortgages back securities that are sold to private investors. This practice allows banks and lenders to clear out their warehouse lines of credit so they have more money available to lend to other homeowners.

Freddie Mac: A program similar to Fannie Mae designed to help those with low or moderate incomes, including first-time homebuyers, who obtain mortgage financing through their lenders.

Federal Housing Administration (FHA): A division of the Department of Housing and Urban Development (HUD); guarantees loans to lenders under certain conditions to allow those who may not otherwise qualify for a mortgage to obtain one. The FHA program is primarily for first-time homebuyers, with little down payment and higher debt ratios.

Foreclosure: The legal procedure whereby a lender takes possession of the property placed as collateral on the loan by the mortgage due to a default in payments.

Hazard/homeowner's insurance: Covers damage to or loss of the property. If the property is mortgaged, the lender is listed as the mortgagee on the policy.

Index: The financial instrument that is the basis for the interest rate on an adjustable rate program.

Interest: A finance charge collected in addition to the repayment of principal; a cost of the loan.

Interest credit: A lender credit for interest from the first day of the month through the funding date. The first payment will be due on the first of the next month.

Loan-to-value (LTV): The loan amount divided by the appraised value (or sales price on a purchase). The difference is the equity in the property (or the down payment in a purchase). **CLTV**, combined loan-to-value includes the second mortgage, if applicable.

Locking an interest rate: Assigning an interest rate to a loan, committing the lender to lend the specified amount of money at the specified rate.

Margin: The spread, which when added to the index, determines the interest rate.

Mortgage: The recorded document placing a lien on the property based upon the terms of the note. (The mortgage is not the same as the note.)

Non-permanent resident alien: A non-U.S. citizen temporarily in the United States on a visa for work or pleasure.

Note: The document that obligates the borrower to repay the loan, detailing the terms, including rate, repayment period, and prepayment penalty (if any).

Par interest rate: The base interest rate which neither costs the borrower nor pays the loan officer.

Payment shock: The difference between the new mortgage payment and the current rent or mortgage payment.

PITI: Principal, interest, taxes, insurance; the total mortgage payment with escrows.

Point: One percent of the loan amount.

Prepaid interest: Interest collected at closing from the funding date through the end of the month because the first payment will be made on the first of the second month to pay the principal and accrued interest for the first full month.

Private mortgage insurance (PMI): Coverage provided by a mortgage insurance company to protect the lender from losses incurred if the borrower defaults on the mortgage loan. PMI is usually required if the first mortgage is more than 80 percent of the sales price (purchase) or appraised value (refinance).

Sales contract: A written document specifying the terms of the sale of real estate between a buyer and seller.

Seasoned funds: Money that has been in an account at least sixty days is considered the borrower's own funds. If the money came from a loan, sixty days should be enough time for the debt to show on the credit report.

Secondary financing: Second mortgage that is subordinate to the first mortgage.

Sourced funds: Documentation showing where the money to close comes from—two months' bank statements showing the money in the borrower's account is considered sourced. Tax refunds and cash from the equity on real property are acceptable sources, among others.

Survey: A drawing of the property showing boundary lines, any improvements, easements, and building setback lines. The survey also shows any encroachments of structures over any easements or property lines.

Title insurance: Covers the insured against title problems; usually obtained at the closing of a purchase. Lender's coverage is mandatory if the property is financed. Owner's coverage is optional, but important to the owner and should be obtained.

Veterans Administration: Guarantees loans for lenders made to qualified veterans or veteran's spouses. The VA will charge a funding fee to the veteran/spouse that replaces private mortgage insurance. The funding fee may be rolled into the loan amount.

Warehouse lines of credit: A lender's revolving line of credit that the lender uses to fund real estate mortgage loans.

Yield spread: "Back points," expressed as a percentage of the loan amount paid to the broker for locking interest rates higher than par.